GOD,
if you have a
plan for my life,
where were
you last
Thursday?

and other stories from Jess Moody

by

JESS MOODY

B&H
BROADMAN
&HOLMAN
PUBLISHERS

Nashville, Tennessee

0-8054-2394-X

Published by Broadman & Holman Publishers, Nashville, Tennessee

Dewey Decimal Classification: 242
Subject Heading: CHRISTIAN LIFE—ANECDOTES
Library of Congress Card Catalog Number: 2001025353

Unless otherwise stated all Scripture citation is from the KJV, The King James
Version. Other versions cited are TLB, The Living Bible, copyright © Tyndale
House Publishers, Wheaton, Ill., 1971, used by permission; AMP, The Amplified
Bible, Old Testament copyright © 1962, 1964 by Zondervan Publishing House,
used by permission, and the New Testament © The Lockman Foundation 1954,
1958, 1987, used by permission; The New English Bible, © The Delegates of the
Oxford University Press and the Syndics of the Cambridge University Press,
1961, 1970, reprinted by permission.

Library of Congress Cataloging-in-Publication Data
Moody, Jess.
   God, if you have a plan for my life, where were you last Thursday? / Jess
Moody.
      p. cm.
   ISBN 0-8054-2394-X (pb.)
      1. Christian life—Anecdotes. 2. Christian life—Baptist authors. I. Title
   BV4517.M666   2001
   242—dc21   2001025353
                                                              CIP

1 2 3 4 5 6 7 8 9 10 04 03 02 01

Dedication

To my beloved Doris.
I cannot organize two rocks and was destined
to the world of inconsideration.
She could organize the Pentagon!
I love her dearly.

Preface

I have become convinced that we are so bombarded by the sensates and an inundation of verbal baptism that we cannot speak and be understood except by opening the windows and letting the sunshine of stories flow through.

Two hundred years ago we were ignorant because of a lack of learning. Today we are ignorant because of the flood of sensate emotions, sounds, advertising—a blitzkrieg of babble. It has rendered our age devoid of the ability to comprehend; ergo, we are drowning in postmodern ignorance.

For every ounce of philosophy, there is a pound of computerese. We are worshiping the gods ROM and RAM, and we are smitten by megabytes. Piranalike, they are eating us alive.

People are drowning in multicolored printer's ink—and the inkwell is deeper and wider than we can negotiate. Man is communicating through multitudes of modern megaphones:

Internet, telephones, Palm Pilots, and Intel, ad infininitum, ad regurgitatum.

This has made the original way of communication unique. With thousands of electronic whirls and whizzes, gewgaws and gadgets, human speech spinning a simple yarn is quaint but quite the *in thing* to do! If you don't believe this, try counting the money the *Chicken Soup* books have made.

We live in a world much akin to the first century. The acids of modernity have eaten away our sophistication, and we are stripped down to the nakedness of simplicity. Only the fig leaf of respectability allows us to walk the streets of the screeching brakes of conservative screams and the hoarsened gripes of ignored dinosaurian liberals.

The world is filled with a cacophony of cries of unmet needs, squelched requests, and verbal vomit from ego intoxication—and humankind is like a tired, but sleepless child, desperately in need of a calming, simple, Jesuslike story.

My prescription for your overloaded spirit is a soul-calming or life-challenging little story.

This may be the last functional form of real communication left.

By the way, giving literary credit where due: I learned this technique from the greatest storyteller of all time, Jesus of Nazareth, who would say to the broiling sea of sensates:

"Peace, be still!"

Table of Contents

The Book Inside of Me

Just think!
There is a book inside me, aching to come out.
I've tried to determine where it hides.
If it's in my left brain, it might be a philosophical tome.
If it's in my right brain, a book about celebrative dancing.
If it is in my lungs, it could end up a windy sermon book.
If it lurks in my heart, it could become The Great Love Story.
If it is in my upper intestine, a saga of great courage.
If it hides in my kidneys, a cynical, critical essay.
If it prowls in my bowels, an R-rated movie.

Whatever.

It still lies somewhere within me.
No one can read it until is born.
No unborn book has ever been read.

For heaven's sake, don't gestate forever!
A book unwritten is tombstone gone,
For all practical purposes, it might as well be dead.
So I have nudged my deepest self,
To spout out from my mind
Through my fingers, to the pen, to the page
With adjectival alacrity,
And hemorrhaging logorrheic outpouring.
So come, alphabet!
Come, ready pen!
Come verbal colors: red, black, pink, and purple!
Come sizzling words,
Give me marching, moving verbs.
Give me nouns, front and back o' me
words, Words, WOrds, WORds, WORDS!
Describing galaxies that hypnotize
And give paralyses,
And infinite infinitives,
Commixed with genitives
To possess and squeeze
Till we cough and wheeze
The words, Words, WOrds, WORds, WORDS!
No verbosity,
No pomposity—
Just plain old WORDS!!!

Well, I've put a few of them together
In this strange little book;
With the hope that you'll all give it

a loving, charitable look;
And looking, see and feel
Or perhaps pray, communicate
and kneel . . .

Introduction

Before you read this book, please read this.

Jesus would have flunked a modern speech writing course.

Left-brained, outline-prone speakers bore the bejabbers out of the average listener.

The reason Jesus shines so brightly, even in the secular mind, is that the world remembers his deathless stories.

I am a storyteller and have been since I won a district story-telling contest when I was in the second grade. My gifts are limited, but I can tell a story.

Thoroughly researched, well-documented tomes of heavy intelligence are remembered but a short while, but stories have legs and can run a mile while a position paper is putting on its shoes.

I have been collecting stories for fifty-five years, and I have thousands of them.

This book is a look at life as it really is, and as good people want it to be, revealed in the pure down-home goodness, bleeding, dying, cheering, hurting and healing, warts-and-all stories about facing hard realities, death, and taxes. There is a strain of faith running through these stories, as well as death as an incident in life rather than an accident. Here is hope commingled with love, fun, justice—all running down the hill of life like a flood!

I wanted to call this book *Hallewhoopee!* because I have had an overdose of hallelujahs with the sheer fun of whoopee! In other words, life is supposed to be lived with intense spirituality and a huge dose of perfect naturalness thrown in! I was born excited and never had a relapse.

For my readers, may this book give you enough spiritual excitement to make it possible to ride the river of life from here to heaven's streets of gold!

Having written it from a Chinese viewpoint—death infers life, darkness pleads for light, and despair is the brother of joy—I ask the reader to believe these stories, and never lose your childlike wonder that knows there is wonder after wonder . . .

. . . AND EVERY WONDER IS TRUE!!!

The streets of America are paved with hot asphalt.
The streets of New Jerusalem are
paved with transparent gold.
Jesus Christ teaches us how to walk on *both!*

ONE

Dorcas Everly's Two Hours in Heaven

Owensboro, Kentucky, is large enough to feel like a city but small enough to have that hometown feel.

I was the green, young minister at the First Baptist Church, trying to make that fairly large congregation offer meaning and hope to its people. Offering that meaning for everyone was a far greater task than my abilities could accommodate, so much so that I felt like a person who had just soloed in a Piper Cub and moved immediately to the cockpit of a jet fighter. There were so many instruments glowing out at me, so many levers to push or pull, so many buttons to punch, that I often had to fly by the seat of my pants.

There are realities of human nature that will teach a young pastor in a hurry. I was about as clumsy as a giraffe doing ballet, but I was on stage and had to perform. Fortunately, there were understanding people who tolerated my clumsiness and honed my gifts.

There was a beautiful young lady and her handsome husband, Dorcas and Carl Everly. They had two children, and Dorcas was what would now be called a budding soccer mom. They were about our age, and Doris and I gravitated to them. They were openhanded and openhearted to us. We liked them a lot. They were quite kind to us, and the relationship grew rather rapidly.

I would tell Carl, "We married the two best-looking women in town, didn't we?"

"Not in this town—in this *state!!*" Carl would reply.

We did love our two beautiful ladies.

One day, I was in the swarm of morning duties at the church office, and Carl called.

"Hey, what's up, big Carl?"

"Jess, it's Dorcas. She has cancer—advanced stages—won't make it for long, they say."

I walked into the hospital room and met the most glowing face I had ever seen. Have you ever seen anything more beautiful than a thirty-year-old woman, looking brave in the face of adversity? This Christian woman, under such a struggle, holding up; and her basket-case husband over in the corner. I've seen that so often that it is now a given.

I was fresh out of miracles, so I gave the only thing I could, my tears. There was no need for the baloney of bravado-masked-as-faith that smiles and gives assurance that everything will be all right.

I thought that shedding tears right in front of people who needed a confident minister was quite disgraceful. *A fine jerk of a pastor, you are, Moody. They need Scripture, faith, glowing assurance, hope, and confidence. And you stand there blubbering and staggering. Get out of the ministry, and get a job that doesn't make demands on your emotions, something like a parole officer or a typist.*

They told me later that tears minister better than words.

I had learned in the seminary from Dr. Wayne Oates about logotherapy; but I later was told that tearotherapy is better.

Days went by with inexorable turtleness. Dorcas had been reduced to a frail shell, laboring for breath, still smiling when I came into the hospital room.

I received a call from nurse Godzilla, a huge hunk of reality, one of those who cuts to the chase before the chase ever starts.

"Dorcas wants you to come over alone. She has something to tell you."

She hung up, without a good-bye.

"Thank you, Miss Blunt," I said to the dead phone. "You belong at the ER in the Bronx."

I wondered what a dying beauty queen would say to me.

I walked in the door. Dorcas smiled at me wanly, radiating as much light as she could from her sunken eyes.

"Jess, yesterday I heard you on the radio, and you said that a day is unto the Lord as a thousand years, and a thousand years is as a day."

I interrupted her with that you-mustn't-overdo word.

"Hush, and listen for once, Jess. I want to be the preacher for a minute."

You clumsy jerk, let her talk, I thought.

"Well, I tried to figure that out, and it seems that if a day is as a thousand years, then an hour is forty years."

She was wheezing out the words, straining with each breath.

"I will be leaving Carl and the children soon. He will probably live another forty years. I will be in heaven when he arrives, and I will say, 'Carl, where have you been? I haven't seen you for an hour. Did you run out to Papa's farm?'"

She then gripped my tie and pulled me in closer.

"The children will live, maybe, another eighty years. That will be two hours for me. I will greet them, and hug them, and say, 'Children, how was school today? When you are gone from me for two hours, I wonder how things are with you. Mommies don't like to be away from their children for long.'"

In a few days Dorcas was gone.

At the funeral Carl told me that she had said to him at the hospital, just before she died: "Carl, I love you. Take care of my kids. I'll see you in an hour."

TWO

An Explanation to My Kids

I am keeping up my interest by making tiny purchases on eBay.

The U.S. Mint has released the "Medals of the Presidents" series. I bid low and got it! It is a coin on every president in U.S. history. Beautiful, well presented in a case. A picture of a president on one side of the shimmering golden coin and a quote or etching on the other.

Another feature of my weird tastes: I now have a complete set of watch fobs, each with a major railroad line featured: Southern Pacific, Canadian National, MKT, SOO, Illinois Central, Santa Fe, and many others.

I'll bet a dollar to a doughnut that you can ask fifteen people under forty to tell you what a watch fob is, and they can't tell you.

I can still hear the lonesome night wail of those old trains, at 3:00 A.M. in West Texas in the 1930s. It is one of those sounds that brings a tear to an old man's eye. Hard to explain.

They look great on my watches. I have one watch made in 1809 in Birmingham, England; and it still runs perfectly.

Amazingly, the ones that run the best are the old dollar watches. There was the Enduro, the Westclox, and the Ingersoll. I have two Westclox Pocket Bens and a Westclox Scotty. They still run perfectly and are now worth about fifty dollars apiece.

I remember that I was so proud when, on my ninth birthday, Dad plunked down seventy-nine cents at Stokes Drug Store for a new Ingersoll that was "on sale." If cared for, it would still be running today.

In Galilee in the second century, the Christian apologist Justin Martyr said that during his lifetime it was still common to see farmers using plows made by the carpenter Jesus of Nazareth.

Think about it: the second Person of the triune Godhead spent much of his earthly life working in a wood shop. By that act alone God forever established the significance of *our* work in this world.

I want to explain my fascination with old watches.

There is not a company today that could make one of these things. It would take $1,000,000 to make from scratch an Elgin like my 1872 "biscuit." Incidentally, it is the same type watch Lincoln was wearing at the Ford Theater *that* night. His can be seen in Springfield, Illinois, at the Lincoln Museum.

Today they do not know how to make something that will run for one hundred years simply by winding it every day.

Today things are built to break down after a short time so the economy may be kept up.

Like Vance Packard's *Throwaway Society.*

Our washer and dryer just broke down here at the condo in Palm Beach.

"They don't make parts for these anymore. You'll have to buy a new one."

I know it's good for the economy, but it is terrible for integrity.

I want you to see why I am collecting things that can't be duplicated. I am still astounded that I have a watch like that one Dad gave me, which cost seventy-nine cents sixty-five years ago, and it's still going.

Like the Energizer Bunny.

THREE

The Day Dad Met Jesus

Father's Day is a favorite day in my life. It gives me a chance to talk about my dear dad. Horace Moody was like Gary Cooper, the strong silent type, who watched life with the eye of an eagle as it passed by.

He liked to be called "The Old He," I think because there was a mixture of mystery, Indian blood, and quiet strength in that title. He said little, worked hard, loved his wife dearly, and was proud of his son, though he seldom told me so.

I played football for three years. He never attended a game the entire time, until one night when we played a tough game against Bay City. I played my heart out the whole game, hoping to please him. After the game, I asked, "Dad, how did I do?"

He said, "I dunno. Which one were you?"

He wasn't a Christian, and we were all concerned for his soul. One day Dad—quite ill—said, "Son, can you teach me how to plug in?" I knew what he meant, so I told him how to find Jesus as his Savior. He quietly bowed his head and gave his life to the Lord Jesus.

Mother came roaring out of the kitchen, shouting praise to the Lord. She had prayed for him for more than forty years. We all danced around the room in a dizzying dervish of delight.

Shortly after that Dad's stately steps walked to, as he called it, "my final home."

I can hardly wait to see that old silent character again.

I am certain that *there,* he won't ask, "Which one were you?"

FOUR

Breakfast with a 2000-Year-Old Man

I couldn't have been more shocked if I had heard that Louis Farrakan were dating Mother Theresa.

What shocks me? The New Age movement. All bubblegum and Yellow Brick Road. All ecstasy; no agony. No pain—all gain. Going through life like the Von Trapp family, dancing and singing through the hills, while hard reality is wrenching the guts out of people on the battlefield of the hot streets of the modern secular city.

They burn no bridges. They don't even singe them. New Age people, lecturing for three hundred dollars a seat, teach that the poor street people deserve it. It's their karma, you see.

But for the Malibu, Santa Fe, New Age crowd, rainbows circle their heads, lemon drops and gentle ocean spray, a kiss from good Mother Earth, and the cancer goes away.

The garish, the perverted, constantly reinventing themselves and reimagining the landscape. The bizarre, the interesting but irrelevant. The palace is burning down, and Shirley MacLaine flies to the moon and plays among the stars. I hope the umbilical holds while she scans Jupiter and Mars. And Seattle people huddle in shadowy little dives and animatedly discuss their previous lives.

Movie producers, tired of feeling that no production ever went broke overestimating the stupidity of the average movie-goer, have found a new *Star Wars, E.T.,* and *Star Trek.*

This New Age religion beats all of them. One can travel through time by reincarnation—no spaceships, no set costs, no mock-ups. Just here is the person, there is the person. Shazzamm! Bingo! Zapp! You are in another life!

The New Agers are now in the process of writing their doctrines. The reason I know the movement will die rapidly is that they have written their system of beliefs so terribly fast.

It took the Christians sixteen hundred years to get most of it down. These theological jokers barfed their beliefs in three years' time. It is a loosely tied knot, oversimplifying every-thing. Too many robot responses to and through the maze of the human dilemma.

As I said, all bubblegum and Yellow Brick Road.

Our Christian faith took thousands of martyrdoms in the Circus Maximus in Rome.

Their idea of martyrdom is a sore arm from pulling the slot machines in Circus Circus in Las Vegas.

Our martyrs' blood ran knee-deep on the horses.

Theirs is wading ankle deep in the cold waters of Paradise Cove.

A Savanarola, dying in the fire.

A Shirley Mac, standing on a beach, screaming, "I am god! I am god!"

A Latimer and Ridley cooked in the streets of Oxford.

A clutch of the Committed unto the Holy Crystals in the streets of Sedona, Arizona, dedicated to be loyal till the end of the tourist season.

A Joan of Arc's last low moans.

A few chanters, throwing bones.

We aren't writing *Sesame Street* here, for God's sake! We are making history here, for Christ's sake!

Their talks, for which people pay three hundred dollars a seat, where they criticize some TV evangelists for raising money to buy TV time. Then, when they really get down deep, their messages are a light salad, no dressing, no potatoes, no meat—and their drink is hogwash.

A people's belief system will never amount to much if talking with them is like having a happy puppy breathe over his salivating tongue into your newly licked clean countenance.

As I said, they don't burn bridges. They don't even singe them.

All of the above is why I was hesitant to accept a breakfast with a man whose name I shan't reveal because he asked me not to mention it.

He is a channeler. One of those people who claim that he is one through whom someone from a long-distant past time comes back, using a present timer's body and voice.

I call it *trans temporal ventriloquism.* You know what that is—when someone speaks through a dummy.

Of course, I didn't convey these definitions to the gentleman who called me, hypocrite that I am.

"Where shall we meet?"

He seemed insistent.

I have taken and taught courses on personal witnessing; but there just wasn't a chapter in any of the books on how to witness to a guy through whom someone who predated Christ used a body of a latter-twentieth-century human being to speak to me. There just ain't nothing in those books like that! It seemed like a propitious time to worry and pray. Witnessing to him would be like frisking a wet seal. So I played a subtle trick on him.

Most New Age stuff is nothing but baptized, Americanized Hinduism, rephrased in evangelical terms.

"How about 'The Wholly Cow' restaurant? It's off the 118 Freeway, north on Tampa—the little shopping center on the right."

"That sounds *wonderful!*"

Somehow I knew that he would react positively to *that* suggestion.

My eyes searched the little restaurant in the mini-mall for this semi-swami, with a viaduct countenance.

Let's call him Kevin.

A not unhandsome man, in his early forties, waved me over: polo shirt, ice cream trousers, alligator shoes (My mind thought that odd. Who knows, he might be wearing a relative!), no socks. On his left pinkie he wore a nearly feminine amethyst ring, which was masculinized by a gold football on a golden chain around his neck. Mixed messages everywhere!

His obviously doctored white teeth, given brilliance by his deeply tanned face, flashed friendly.

Kevin looked pretty good, contrasted to my glorious girth, wallowing around in my rugby shirt and dockers, and weighing down my Reebocks. I felt outgunned.

We played volleyball with banalities for a while. Finally, I shifted past the light lobs over the net.

"Since Hollywood is into its three favorite pastimes: cocaine, past lives, and Baptist bashing, how come you want to see me? I am a Baptist. You want to bash?"

He wasn't taken aback by my query. "We are so far apart in our ideology, I just wanted to find out what made you tick—a person with such an odd and unusual philosophy of life."

I thought, *Zowie! Has it really come to this, that Baptists, one of the three major philosophies of life that molded Jefferson, Washington, and Madison, have come to appear odd in the United States? Baptists, progenitors of the ideals that are shaking the daylights out of China, Russia, and Eastern Europe. Are we Baptists failing here?*

Suddenly, I wished to be a channeler myself, so I could let Roger Williams, Isaac Backus, and John Leland straighten this sucker out!

Of course, I said none of this.

He continued: "So I was just wondering what you believe, so I might relate to you and communicate with you the wisdom of the ages." He smiled, with that sickening, "I know something you don't know" look.

This misanthrope, hanging onto Shirley MacLaine's financial umbilical chord, is going to communicate to me the wisdom of the ages! My smiling face hypocritically covered up my countering thoughts.

"But what the hay," he said, quite condescendingly, but beguilingly. "I want to be fair with you."

"Golly, thanks." I said.

I knew he had seen too many movies where Baptist ministers were depicted as no-brainers, hot pants, quick zippers, with bellies full of bigotry.

He continued to intone: "I truly want to know, if you can verbalize it, so I can understand what you believe about God, or the gods."

So I decided to give him a few stumbling words to *try* to communicate from my infertile brain to the man who was the channel of the "wisdom of the ages." I told him I didn't have five minutes for a peekaboo god who wouldn't show us what he was like and left it to the wisdom of the inhabitants of this, one of the lesser planets in the universe, to believe whatever their vastly limited minds wanted to concoct, based on their own enlightened self-interest. And, I told him, I believed there was one true God who created a mathematically precise universe, then clearly revealed exactly who he is, what he wants, and how he wants it done. This kind God did not leave it to the flounderings of my mind. I, being one-six billionth of the population of one small planet in an endless cosmos of billions of planets . . .

I went on to tell this vast reservoir of truth that I believed that a miracle is just God acting naturally, just being himself; that nothing is too hard for him, including revealing exactly what he is like; and that he ceased being some Vast Vapor in space, incomprehensible—thus leaving it to us to create whatever silly little god we wanted to, which is why he clearly defined himself by coming in the one form, one definition we could understand, which is our form, our humanity. That is why Jesus Christ is the only sense that makes any sense, and all other sense, compared to him, is nonsense.

Yes, I believe Jesus Christ was present at the creation of the cosmos, that he spoke worlds into existence, and tumbled universes from his fingertips. This God-in-flesh could quite adequately reveal his vast self to infinitesimally small beings by becoming one of us, which would be no big deal to a God who can create a universe.

I said that Jesus Christ was God lovingly giving us a clear and final definition of himself in order to keep us from thinking, from our grape-seed brains, that one definition of God is as good, accurate, and definitive as another.

I said I believe Jesus Christ is as much God as if he were not man at all and as much man as if he were not God at all. That he is all God and all man, with two wills, two minds, two natures, coeternal, coexistent, coequal with God. He became man by means of a physical birth, with Mary, a fully human Jewish virgin conceiving, by means of the fathering of the child by the instrumentality of the Holy Spirit, the third person of the Trinity.

He raised his hand.

"Right there I trip up," he said. "I just can't accept that virgin birth bit.

"I have sat here, with extreme patience, and listened to your doctrinal dissertation," he said. "May I now tell you what I believe?"

"Say on!" I replied.

Let him speak. After all, I was actually being allowed to converse with, as his billing said, "one of the masters of the universe." I really should grovel in gratitude because I was getting all this info without paying the three hundred clams to sit at his feet!

"I was born in Virginia, raised in a Fundamental (Capital F) Baptist home and church. They preached against dancing, movies, makeup, and moderate drinking. It was hell-fire damnation for breakfast, lunch, and dinner."

I had heard this litany so many times out here in Hollywood that I lip-synched it while he said it.

He went on: "I barfed it lock, stock, and baptistry; then came to California to escape that inflexibility."

Fifty percent of the people in California came here hoping to be discovered. The other 50 percent came hoping they wouldn't be. Kevin was one of those.

His eyes pierced mine with what seemed to be a rehearsed speech-body language combination. I have been in the motion picture business long enough to know that it reeked with technique.

"I searched for meaning, purpose, and self-respect. I searched for God by attending churches all over Los Angeles, seeking these things. Meaning, man, that's what I had to find."

I thought of Victor Frankl's book *Man's Search for Meaning. Here's a classic case,* I thought.

He proceeded. "I never found these things, until one day, I met two wonderful gentlemen who showed me *the way.* After two conversations with them, I was invited—and went—to the home of one of them.

"It was there that this amazing thing happened to me. They told me that I was a very special person, chosen for a very unique work—and would I be willing to trust them as they led me into this beautiful new experience."

"And you yielded to this?" I questioned.

"Not at first. Then, as we chatted, I began to feel more at ease with them."

Familiar pattern, I thought. He had my *undivided* attention, I can tell you.

He continued on recounting this truly fascinating story.

"One of the men, Eric, worked with me, and finally, I went into this hypnotic trance.

"'Go back in time to your very earliest recollections.'

"I went down into the deep caverns of my memory—back, back until I was three years old.

"'That is about as far as I can go,' I told them.

"'Now, here is a very critical juncture in your experience,' they said.

"'It is here that you must show great faith. Now, by faith, go back to your earliest memory, until you come to the time you are warmly housed in your mother's womb. Now, back, back until you are but a sperm. Now, reach beyond that, by faith, and a friendly hand will grip you and take you back into another life, which preexists your present one.'"

I don't mind telling you, he had me *glued* to this conversation.

"Then, I felt this hand escort me into a previous existence. I was in Springfield, Missouri.

"I was led by Eric until I came to my young childhood in Missouri.

"Then, I was on my own. I knew what to do now. I went back into that mother's womb, then back into another and another, until finally I had gone back through thirty-eight lives.

"It is there, there. . . ."

He seemed to get very misty-eyed with awe and wonder shining through his face, in this well-rehearsed presentation.

"It was there . . . there . . ."

Someone was standing there beside me. Was it a spirit . . . or Eric . . . or what? It was the waiter.

"Water, anything else, dessert, or would you like your check?"

"*Puh-lees,* give us a few minutes more."

I had to hear the end of this. After all, this was the first time I had heard a person recounting his serial reincarnations!

Kevin never broke stride, stayed in character. I wondered if this were his "earth job," which is whatever actors can get, while they are waiting to be discovered. Actually, I would call this thing Kevin was doing an "unearthly job."

He continued. "It was there . . . there . . . thirty-eight lives ago, more than eighteen hundred years back, that I met this charming, brilliant self that I was then. He told me all sorts of revelatory truths, insights. He also told me that he was extremely frustrated because he had been given such futuristic wonders to tell; but when he tried to tell them, the people rebelled and stoned him to death.

"I then felt that I should offer him my voice to speak to me, through me, to the people of the twenty-first century."

His face lit up. I thought I detected tears in his eyes, tears of gratitude and hope, that someone might listen to his amazing revelations.

"So that's my story."

He was trembling in the ecstasy of the telling of it, breathing heavily, like a miler who had just crossed the finish line.

"Now then, dear *Dr.* Jess Moody, what do you think of *that?*"

He was beaming confidence across the table.

"I think . . ."

"Yes, yes!" he prompted.

"I think anyone who has spent that much time in that many wombs, over that many years . . . shouldn't have any trouble believing in the virgin birth of Jesus Christ!"

Of course, we finished our conversation amicably. Then we went our separate ways. He, to the North Pole—and I, to the South.

UPDATE!

Kevin's audiences dropped off to nothing. He is now, I am told, selling cars in Oxnard.

The thought hit my mind: Is he taking Cadillacs back in time, through previous existences, . . . back . . . back . . . to when they were wheelbarrows?

FIVE

The Tweaker and the Tweakee

I am a right-brained foolish fool,
Who possesses but one usable tool—
That's seeking what needs to be tweaked.
The tweaking is not my gift.
I point to the tweaker what needs to be tweaked.
If it's left to me to tweak, I'll freak from tweaking.
The art of teaching to find the tweaking
Is a gift so many tweakers are seeking.
So I'll cease seeking to tweak
'Cause to me it's just Greek
This seeking to tweak what needs tweaking!

SIX

An Old Missionary's Dream

Note: The following story is a fictional account.

I was seventy-one, sitting in a plane waiting its turn at the airport. I lay back, put my mind in neutral, and slipped into a wonderful sleep.

The dream:

As of last Thursday, I was eighteen years old.

I graduated from high school last June. I made average grades. I have been working this summer for our county newspaper, a sort of cub reporter for Mr. Shannon, the owner and publisher. He started it thirty years ago and had built it into something of a news-about-nothing-much sort of paper. I have had this title, cub reporter, which when translated means that I go to pick up packages, run to the post office, and deliver papers to those houses where our two paperboys, Fric and Frac, as I call them, failed to hit the porch and lost them in the azaleas.

Mr. Frank Shannon is the typical newspaper editor, wearing a hand-tied bow tie and an old tweedy coat with newspapers bulging out of the pockets. The baggy pants hang limply on his skinny body, held securely by braces, or suspenders, as some people call them. He walks through the streets and is the town squire, the resident intellectual. It is required of such people that they pontificate without having the pontificator's attitude.

A newspaper in a small town like ours is more than a purveyor of news. It is a commentary on the real life of a town. It talks to folks about nothing more than is said around the coffee drinkers at Harvey's Café or the Duck Inn, farther out on the highway.

In fact, the news has picked up in intensity and accuracy since Mr. Frank, as everybody called him, started coffeeing with the Brethren-of-Good-Fellowship-but-Never-Would-Intentionally-Cause-Anybody-Any-Harm Jawing Society.

They did little more than comment to my uncle, Jay, who really owned the place but looked so humble that everyone thought that Mother owned everything. She was Jay's sister-in-love (as he called her), the cashier with the big smile and the ready quip.

Well, I soon learned to listen to Mr. Frank right after he came fresh from the Jawing Society. I learned who was suing whom, renovating a room, drinking Schenley's for zoom, or headed for economic doom.

I thought I might like to own a countywide newspaper someday, but, glamorous as it was, it never seemed quite enough.

Come to think of it, nothing ever seemed quite enough. Not lawyering, coaching, running a business, owning a bicycle shop or a used-car lot—nothing ever seemed enough. There just wasn't enough world-change in anything that occurred to me.

I am eighteen. I not only read our paper, but I also read the *Houston Post.* I read it religiously because I can tell what's coming down in London, Paris, Moscow, or the Sudan—or just everywhere.

A young boy of eighteen, with a lot of desire to mean something in this world, but not knowing where to go, or what to do, really needs somebody to help him think through how to find a handle on changing the world. I hated that stuff about marrying some nice girl here in our town, inheriting somebody's business, keeping it clicking, then leaving it to your kids, who will leave it to their kids. Nuts to that noise! It just isn't for me.

That's for the Billy Hightowers of this world, who seem committed to sit around and listen to the little birds chirp out "same! same! same!" and sit around and try to help pick out a "name! name! name!" for Delbert Gene's kid who is coming in August. I wanted to call him Justin for "just in time!" because he is coming just nine months, one day, and fifteen minutes after they married.

Mind you, there are a lot of fine girls who live here, but eighteen is no time to be thinking of marriage. I can offer a girl very little anyhow. I've been nowhere, don't plan to go anywhere, or do anything much.

I have had an eye for Mary Fair. She's smart, cute, wealthy, wholesome, built right, talks knowledgeably about more than who's-going-to-be-cheerleader-next-year and when is Rotan's store going to get in those bottom-glamorizing jeans and was Virgie really pregnant like she claimed? No, that isn't for Mary Fair.

She really likes me, but who wants a cub reporter from a little rag called the *Spectator,* a guy who doesn't seem to care about much of anything except who makes All American and who has a car to go to the coast to go floundering?

Floundering. That's a good word for me. I'm just lying on my side at bottom, waiting for somebody to stab me into awareness of what's-it-all-about.

Mary Fair is a church girl. And that's fine for her. For me, that will come in time when I am married, have a couple of kids, and one of them gets some kind of disease that nobody knows anything about; and when push comes to shove, then I'll think about God.

But now, with no war to stir my blood patriotism, and no president leading us into anything much, and no prospect of anything happening to me other than getting a job at Mr. Moore's service station when Joe Bill, his boy, goes away to college—I guess I am doomed to mediocrity.

Norton Rugeley graduated with me. He's preparing to be a doctor like his dad.

Prentiss Conway, the oilman's son, is in Princeton, dragging down the grades.

Betty Caulfield is in Hollywood, hoping to make it.

Joe Spikes is at Rice, playing basketball.

Bobby Speil has won an award of some kind for writing something.

They have figured out what they are to do.

Here I am, Chopped Liver, going nowhere fast and gaining more speed. I am progressing into obscurity! Why can't I seem to focus?

Mary Fair has realized this, and I can tell she's getting a bit impatient with me. She says she can't get me to talk about anything much. Last week, at Outlar's Drug, while sitting around with the boys, Jody Jones said he might ask Mary Fair for a date, if I didn't mind. I did mind, but I just sat there and grunted out, "I don't care."

Mary Fair heard about what I said, and stuck the dagger in me.

"I might just go out with him. At least he has ambition to do something with his life!"

That hurt, but I didn't respond to what she said.

I dunno. What can I do to make her see me in a different light? The light she had for me a few weeks ago is beginning to fade. I can tell by her finger drumming, looking out the window, and rolling her eyes. I have to do something to bring her back to me a little.

"Mary Fair, how about our going to church next Sunday?"

She grabbed it like a trout for bait.

"Pick me up at my house next Sunday at 9:00 A.M. We'll go to Sunday school, then church."

She seemed pleased, but I felt that I had joined the army, navy, and air corps of the Lord, with all that 9:00 A.M. business.

I showed up at 9:15, but she showed no anger at my tardiness. After all, it takes a lot of courage for a man of eighteen to face both Sunday school *and* church.

We walked into class together, eyes rolled, whispers abounded, I thought as I came in.

"Look what the cat's drug up that the dog wouldn't have!" Gene Barbee piped.

Mary Fair scowled a scowl at Barbee that would make the coyotes howl.

The teacher walked in. It was Eddie Mays, the best blocking back Wharton High ever produced. I didn't know that he went to church.

He looked like he ate Volkswagens for breakfast. I couldn't see why he needed to be in church. After all, it was for old women, babies, and young women, wasn't it?

He taught a good lesson about how tough Christ had to be to stand up to those lawyers and outwit them. How tough he had to be to cleanse the temple by throwing open the gates of the birds and animals, which were offered for sacrifice, and chasing them out of the place, then standing there—flushed and panting—and roaring, "*You* have made it a den of robbers and thieves."

Way ta go, Jesus! I thought.

I never thought of Christ that way. He always looked so frail, so pallid, like a sick consumptive in the pictures on the Sunday school walls in church when I was a kid.

Then Mays told about Christ facing death.

"I know what it is to face death. When I was at Anzio, we all acted so brave when those bullets were whining six inches from our heads. I wanted to cry like I did when I hurt my thumb as a little kid, but you don't. You just fight till you drop.

"You look over at Jimbo Jones, from Jersey, our platoon's resident comedian, with whom you've been for the last three months of this horrible stuff, and you see half his head is blown away; and you want to cry. You remember his talking about marrying Sally when it was all over.

" 'Brave Jesus, come to this battlefield, and stop all this stuff.'

"He didn't; but I remembered how he stood up to them—and from that I got the courage to stand up to those Goose Steppers.

"Somehow Jesus brought us out. So here I am to tell you that Jesus Christ gave me the stuff to get me home. Teaching this little class is a big deal to me. God brought me out of that so I could tell you to get your life in order. You may have to face more that I did!

"O, God, give me temple-cleansing courage!" he prayed.

Then Ed went into a prayer for what he called "cross-facing courage."

"Jesus, at Bastogne I prayed for courage and the belief that I might make it through. You brought me through a hail of ten thousand bullets, some of which missed me by an inch. I know you have a plan for my life. Help me find it and do it. Amen!"

I was transfixed. For the first time I felt the touch of real manhood for Christ.

Then Mary Fair led me into the sanctuary. I say, "led me into the sanctuary," because I didn't know how to get there from the classroom. I guess a pagan doesn't know how to make it from a Sunday school class to the sanctuary and a Christian does.

I thought the worship service would be OK, but I imagined we'd get a lot of "Gentle Jesus, Meek and Mild" stuff.

The music was kind of a shocker. I must not have been to church in a long time. I didn't remember there being a miniature Glen Miller Band over at the left of the platform. They didn't exactly Chattanooga Choo Choo the place, but the music and the singing were alive, familiar, and more to my experience and taste.

I looked around me during the singing. I saw a couple of BMOCs (Big Men on Campus) from my high school. They were really doing what I guess was some godly grooving on the music. Their heads were turned upward. They were singing vertically, like Somebody up there was listening. They were singing to God—and I sensed their sincerity. I have to admit, it kinda' touched me.

The preacher stood up. It was Youth Sunday. I guess the real pastor was away, or something must have happened to him; and they had to get some guy up there to speak, because he had forgotten to wear a tie! Obviously, when he came, he didn't know he was going to speak that day. He came half-dressed for a preacher.

I thought it was a state law that preachers had to wear a tie—even in the shower!

He began with a statement that shook me to my heels. "You are going through life without a clue as to why you were born. You haven't focused on your life's goal, and you don't know the slightest about what you are going to do. That describes about 75 percent of us.

"Maybe, I can bring your mind into focus with a few facts about our world. Jesus told us that all who do not come to him are lost, and when they die, they will go to hell. I didn't say that. Jesus said it. So don't blow off your secular steam on me about that statement. Take it to him and tell him he didn't know what he was talking about when he said it."

My eyes were glued on him.

He had been reading my mail, or somebody told him I said it last week because that is *exactly* what I had said just a few days before.

I looked at Mary Fair. That duck has probably told him what I had been saying! How dare she drag me in here and let him single me out like that!

I felt buck naked before God.

Ah, but this guy wasn't through with me. Mary Fair had really primed him for my being in church that day.

"Your life is out of focus. No clue what to do. Now I'm going to tell you what God is up to."

Lay it on me, man. I can stand about two hours of this kind of beating. I was bitter.

Two hours? He was through in ten more minutes. But not before he had brought my mind into sharp focus on a fact or two.

"Let's look at our world and see if we can be complacent about it. Can we just float along in the face of the following facts?" (All statistics updated to 1999.)

1. Number of nations in the world: 190
2. Number of ethnos (people groups) in the world: 12,500
3. Total world population: 5.85 billion
4. Number of Christians: 1.9 billion
5. Number of Muslims: 1.0 billion

6. Number of Buddhists: 307 million
7. Number of Hindus:: 700 million
8. Number of American missionaries abroad now: 400,000
9. Number of people born every day: 365,000
10. Number of people who die every day: 147,000
11. Percentage of those who die without Christ: 72 percent
12. Leading causes of death in the world:
    - Infection and parasitic diseases
    - Circulatory
    - Cancer
    - Respiratory diseases
    - Infant deaths
13. Number in poverty: 1.3 billion
14. Number of languages: 6,528
15. Number of languages with a translation of the New Testament: 905
16. Average number of Bibles in average American home: 8
17. Number illiterate: 1.1 billion
18. Number of nations restricting Christian missionary activity: 51
19. Average income in USA: $38,782
20. Average income outside: $6,429
21. Average amount American Christians give annually to world missions: $5

The pastor paused, looked straight at the congregation for a full minute, a minute that had eternity in it.

"He'll take an offering for missions now," I thought.

Wrong.

"You are dismissed," he said, flatly.

We all stood there for a minute, then slowly, silently one by one, we left the building.

That night, I couldn't sleep. I wasn't thinking of Mary Fair, the gang, school. None of that small-town stuff. I was thinking of a world dying without the gospel, a world lost in darkness.

Kids who couldn't read.

Dying kids.

Illiterate kids.

"Five dollars!" I thought out loud.

I found myself awake and on my knees.

"God, I have been a ship without a rudder, compass, or sail. I am mapless, chartless, and without a sextant. Please, there are millions who haven't cared and don't care now. Would you please make me one who cares."

That was a night long years ago, but I will never forget it. Fifty years later I look into the face of my bride of forty-five years.

A thousand African faces look up at us as we board the plane to Lisbon, to Miami, and home. We are all weeping, waving a permanent good-bye.

"Mary Fair, thank you for taking me to church that day!"

The plane roars down the runway, lifts up and skyward, going back to my little town where dreams are born.

SEVEN

The Butterfinger that Saved My Life

I was a ministerial student at Baylor University. America had just come through the most serious challenge to its existence, costing our nation a million young men's lives. Those who came back were miniature Supermen, who had faced two giant colossi nations for "truth and the American way." This resulted in a tsunami of a spiritual awakening, which swept around the nation, igniting the youth of this country with spiritual fire and zeal.

A group of young men were called upon to reach those zealous young people with the gospel. I was one of them.

In one year I received more than a thousand invitations to speak. I felt that this was an open window, and the Scriptures said, "Put ye in the sickle for the harvest is ripe."

I had not fought in the war—due to bad eyesight—felt totally guilty because I wasn't there and determined that nothing could keep me back. Dozens of my friends had died in battle—several from the same high school football team—so I was driven to an almost maniacal frenzy of spiritual zeal. It was payback time.

So I took every opportunity I could to try to be a part of that awakening—even if my classwork suffered. And it did. It was bad stewardship, and I knew it, but the pressure of invitations from all over the world was eating me alive.

Fifty years later I am not sure I would have done it any other way, given the sociological and spiritual context of the time. You just had to have been there. Tom Brokaw picked up on the spirit of the times when he wrote *The Greatest Generation.*

I was as driven as the apostle Paul. For good or ill that's the way it was.

Some Christian businessmen in Houston bought me an airplane, a shining little Luscombe Silvaire. They wanted to increase my effectiveness in traveling from place to place.

I didn't know how to fly, so I crammed into my already hopeless schedule a quickie flying course. I started flying cross-country with only twenty hours of training and flight time. It was an adolescent and stupid thing to do, but God does seem to take care of idiots and fools.

I was shortcutting everything. College. Preaching. Flying. Everything. It almost cost me my life.

This story begins one cloudy morning at four-thirty. Pitch dark.

I inspected my little Luscombe, a little two-seater with only a sixty-five horsepower Lycoming engine, one of the most faithful little engines ever built. It brought me through many tough times.

I was in Jacksonville, Texas, and had to be in class at Baylor at 9:00 A.M. My teacher, Dr. Sara Lowrey, didn't give a fig about my worldwide evangelistic fervor. She had a mission also. Teach me how to deliver a speech. After all, I was speaking about three times a day in those youth meetings.

This put the pressure on me to make that class. I could feel her hot breath on my neck to get there.

So, I cranked the prop. The faithful little Lycoming burst into power, shattering the silence of the morning quiet.

I climbed into the cockpit, said my prayer, warmed her up, and took off into the absolute pitch-black sky.

A kind of warm glow settles in when you are flying into the darkness. The reflection of the very few instruments is your only source of light. It can be a deadly hypnosis, such a false sense of security.

My false sense of peace was shattered about ten minutes into that flight. I was confronted with a deadly terror that had taken the lives of scores of amateur pilots, especially those with so few hours of training and experience.

It was so dark that I failed to see a giant wall of fog dead in front of me. I was enveloped before I knew it. I had read horror stories about even seasoned pilots, flying well-equipped planes, who died under the same circumstances.

There I was, a green kid, flying a plane with no T and B—turn and bank indicator—no radio, and no visibility. Old-fashioned postal pilots, like Lindbergh, flying those old Jennys, would tie ribbons on their wing struts to indicate the climb and attitude of the plane toward the horizon, and I didn't even have that. It was a grim situation.

I was trapped in a monstrous fog with few instruments and no experience. A twenty-one-year-old postpubescent, post-acne kid scared out of his wits. It seemed a propitious time to pray.

"Lord, I am on the brink of losing my orientation. I don't have a clue about what to do. Please, in the name of Jesus, help me."

I listened.

Nothing. Just the steady hum of little Lycoming.

Plenty of gas. No visibility.

In a situation like this, the greatest danger is the loss of the sense of up and down, left and right bank, and relation to the horizon. You try to fly by the seat of your pants. It is almost always fatal.

I thought of my parents, Doris, my friends in the youth movement, and thousands of kids coming to Christ. I hadn't been in battle during the war. This was one battle I didn't want to miss!

I yelled, "Brains, don't leave me now!"

I sat there a long minute, then took my hands off the stick. (Yes, *stick,* not wheel—that's how long ago it was!) I noticed that my airspeed was increasing. I was going down, but I didn't sense that sort of movement.

"Act against your feelings!" I commanded myself.

I pulled back on the stick and felt the seat pressure of coming out of a dive. I began to climb, and the airspeed began to slow down.

"Mustn't put her in too much of a climb. Might stall and spin out. Then it's bye-bye, birdy!"

The seriousness of this was compounding by the second. I shook my head to clear out the cobwebs.

"OK, Just you and me, Jesus, right? Look around, Jess, what do you see? Think! Think!"

My eyes surveyed the cockpit. Compass—still headed west. Altimeter—3,100 feet and climbing slightly.

"Remember the crosswinds were at ten knots out of the north. Correct your compass for that. You have been flying for about thirty minutes at about ninety per, so you should be about forty-five to fifty miles west of Jacksonville. This fog is so thick that you can't do the old drop-down-low-and-read-the-water-tower trick."

Funny, how your mind gallops at a time like this.

"Think, Dummy, think!"

I looked over the cockpit a second time.

There were my textbooks, notebooks, my field glasses, a sandwich, a Butterfinger candy bar, my legal pad, my . . .

Wait a minute! A Butterfinger. That *might* do it. I fumbled around the cockpit . . . on the floor, in the seat, then into the glove compartment . . . a few small items, some maps, and a string about eighteen inches long.

Understand, I am about the most antitech klutz around. I think of a wheelbarrow as intricate machinery.

I could have never thought of the idea on my own—not in two millennia.

"Lord, what do I do?"

I looked at the string and thought, *Maybe if I tie this string to that overhead bar and tie it to the middle of that Butterfinger bar, making it a see-saw.* I performed the operation.

"Now, if the Butterfinger swings forward, I am diving. If it swings backward toward me, I am climbing . . . or to the right, I am banking right . . . or left, banking left."

Voila! A perfect T and B!

Some fly in by Norad. I flew in by Butterfinger.

As I came into Dr. Lowrey's class, right on time, she said, "I want four of you to speak spontaneously on the subject 'My Most Exciting Moment.' Emerson, Kurtz, Moody, and White. You will each have five minutes to speak. I will give you five minutes to think about it."

I raised my hand.

"Yes, Mr. Moody."

"I'm ready now, Miss Lowrey."

EIGHT

Voni Lynn and the Tokyo Earthquake

To Voni Lynn Wong, beautiful young member of our Shepherd of the Hills Church, killed in the earthquake, Kobe, Japan, January 17, 1995. This was one year to the day after the Los Angeles earthquake damaged our church. Thirteen thousand homes were destroyed, including our parsonage. I wrote this little tribute from a heart that was sick about her death. The beautiful stained-glass window over the foyer of the church is dedicated to her memory.

VONI LYNN

As I walked the midnight streets
And felt the kiss of a million stars,
My thoughts went out to Voni Lynn
And her joyous beginning again.

I shed a lonely tear or two,
As I thought of this life without you
That is, here and now; now and here,
That's why I shed this lonely tear.

And I could hear her chuckle bright,
"Now, there'll be no tears—not tonight!
Just great vibes, dear Pastor Panda Bear,
And the smile I used to see you wear.

"Because if you knew where I am living—
In the land of love, joy, and forgiving—
You'd shed that tear, it's strangely true;
Not for me, but for them—and you!"

NINE

Gandy and the Big Leaguers

The hospital lights were low.

Gandy had been ill for a long time. A rare form of cancer, they said it was. He had lost most of his hair because of chemotherapy.

The hat he wore made him look girlish—mostly because he had such a beautiful face. The ten-year-old still showed a bit of ire when some new nurse mistook him for a girl.

"I'm not a girl. I am a boy—and someday I'll play ball for the San Francisco Giants—or at least the Dodgers—and I'll pitch so well the manager will give me the game ball. You just wait and see!"

Every employee of the Holy Spirit Hospital in Fort Lauderdale soon knew and loved Gandy. Spunk flowed from his every pore.

Across town, I was speaking to a gathering of Christian athletes at the Yankee Clipper hotel. It was a rousing, wonderfully joyous meeting of laughter and fun.

I had had a great time and was shaking hands with several of the really famous athletes, mostly baseball greats and not so greats. Two of the really greats were Bobby Richardson, the sensational second baseman, and Al Dark, the great player then manager of the Giants.

Bobby said, "Jess, Al and I have to run up to a hospital to meet a little kid they say isn't going to make it very long. Would you like to come along with us?"

I was delighted.

Richardson drove, and we talked about a lot of stuff but mainly about Christ in their lives. These men played to win, and they witnessed to win.

None of this, "Well, let's see, er, (clear the throat) uh" nervousness about speaking up for Christ. Jesus flowed from their lips as easily as they said, "Would you pass the salt, please."

They weren't unfamiliar with the Savior, to say the least. It put even more spine in this preacher!

We entered Gandy's room. He was sitting up in bed, blowing bubbles and swatting at them with his other hand, then quietly and weakly laughing. When he saw us enter, his face lit up like a Christmas tree.

"Bobby Richardson! Al Dark! Wow!"

He was so excited. His little body was literally bouncing in his bed.

Bobby spoke. "We just came up here to see you because we heard you were a big fan—and that you planned to play in the bigs someday."

Then Bobby and Al talked to him for ten minutes or so about what it means to become a Christian. One of the greatest moments in my life was to see those legends of baseball leading a small boy to a saving knowledge of Jesus Christ. I nearly lost it when Bobby led Gandy in a prayer of faith in Christ.

As I looked in on the scene, when Bobby asked Gandy to follow him in prayer, Gandy did something that nobody in the hospital could get him to do. He removed his hat.

Tears rolled down his mother's face—and mine—as I held her hand while they prayed.

Just before they left, Al Dark handed him an autographed baseball.

"This is for being a greater champion than we will ever be—a champion in the only game that really counts, the Game of Life!"

As we walked down the hall, I put my arms around those two tight-muscled men, burst into tears, and said, "I have had one of the greatest experiences of my life tonight. You guys have made me a better preacher than ever before. Thanks. Thanks so much!"

A few days later, I was told that Gandy had died.

It was a beautiful service. As we walked by the small casket, I looked in, and there lay Gandy with the autographed ball in his hand!

Just as he had predicted, the manager, Al Dark, had handed him the game ball for being the most outstanding player in the most important game of all—the Game of Life!

TEN

Where Is Virgil?

Frank and Marilyn Wilson were well-washed, overly insured Republicans. Middle class, some money in savings, they were clamoring for the good life, with enough money to maintain community respectability. Wanting a child to see what that was like, and not to appear selfish, they soon had a boy, whom they named Virgil, after a favorite financial adviser friend.

They lived in an average-to-upper house in an average-to-upper neighborhood, drove small Cads, Devilles. His was rather new, and hers, a little older.

Frank made Rotarian the first try out, and Marilyn was on the board of the country club and president of her missionary society at church. He was a tweedy, horn-rimmed dollar chaser with an alligator briefcase to match his shoes. He rose up the corporate ladder by stepping over the slower climbers in a mad rush to win the contest for the free trip for two to Kauai.

They both avoided drugs and maintained the equipoise needed to be Mr. and Mrs. Happy Twosome of the community. Whatever was good and upbuilding would find Frank and Marilyn's name on the sponsors' list.

They even organized a Bible study in their home, taught by Bob Hamrick, the community Bible whiz. He was so sharp, he even knew that Hezekiah wasn't a book in the Old Testament—and things like that.

Virgil was into, on top of, under, and beside everything. Cub Scouts, sang in the children's choir, made school patrol, sometimes a pain in the gluteus maximus of the family, sometimes so angelic one wondered how he hid his wings. Little League outfielder, good field, big bat, and hustle king. His room featured unfinished model airplanes, trophies, pictures of rock stars, class pics—all of which looked gooney to him and just precious to Mother.

Virgil was fixated on his mother. She was his end-all, be-all, do-all. Mom healed hurts, wished off warts, chauffeured to all little-boy events. Attender at PTA, church-taker, mender of rips, healer of strawberries on the knee, kisser-away of tears, giver of secret money to buy gewgaws which Virgil fancied, soccer mom, approver of haircuts, breath checker, dentist taker, hurrier upper, heartbreaker, homemaker, and punishment administrator.

Mom.

Virgil never could quite figure out who came first, Mom or Jesus.

One day Virgil was wrestling with his dad, with all the laughter, roughhousing, and head-knocking that wrestling entails. The noise was at a decibel gauge's peak.

Marilyn was laughing at the medium of bonding that she felt dad and boy needed, when suddenly she let out a pain-yelp that startled the two ruffians on the rug. She doubled up on the floor and was almost immediately comatose.

Dr. Traylor came out of the ER at the hospital to tell Frank that it looked pretty dark. The X rays showed a giant tumor on the brain, and surgery couldn't do much about it. The doctor and Frank didn't know that Virgil was all ears and heard Dr. Traylor's almost whispered report.

Most often young boys don't scream out and cry openly when such news is given. They simply retreat into the quietness of their room and think a lot—usually looking at the ceiling for a long time. That is what Virgil did.

After a while, they prepared a bed in the den for Marilyn, where the warming rays of the sun could radiate through. It was midsummer, and that room seemed a little cooler.

Virgil learned to be quiet when he was in the house. Everybody was busy there. The nurse and the overnight patient-sitter were extremely efficient. Frank had seen to that.

One day Dr. Traylor stopped by, and after examining Marilyn, talking briefly with the nurse, and Frank, he started to leave without saying anything to Virgil. As he came out on the front porch, Virgil cornered him, saying, "Dr. Traylor, I want to know when my mom's going to go to heaven."

The doctor said the usual things to reassure Virgil that there "may be some new breakthroughs," etc.

"Doctor, how long does my mother have to live? When is she going to die?" Virgil wasn't about to be put off. This was time for judgment-bar honesty.

"Virgil, I suspect that your mother will get to meet Jesus about the time the leaves fall off the trees." With that he was gone.

It was an unusually hot summer. Frank paid special attention to his boy, the ball game bits, the Scout meetings, the whole smear.

Dad was clumsy at listening, and Virgil didn't want to talk to anyone but Mom. He would stand beside her still form and say things like, "Got two hits, today, Mom! I got old smarty pants, Greenwood, out three times. Made him so mad, he called me names! I knew I had him when he blew his cork, because he has a short fuse anyway! I'm doing better in school, much better. I want you to be proud of me, Mom!"

Frank couldn't stand that daily ritual. It went on all summer.

Fall weather was beginning to peekaboo around the clouds, the heated nights cooled remarkably, and mornings had that fresh chilled feeling.

One of those chilly mornings Virgil was going to school. As he walked out the door, his face was hit by a leaf, falling from the poplar tree in the front yard. He turned and ran back into the house.

The school checker called their home to say that Virgil was not in school that day. Frank knew he had walked out the door to go to school. He drove the Caddy around the entire neighborhood. No sign of Virgil.

This was the morning Dr. Traylor was to come by. Frank contained his fears about Virgil's whereabouts, as he talked with the doctor. It was almost Marilyn's *time,* and the doctor had to talk frankly.

"Let's slip out this back door. I have something to tell you, Frank."

It was time for the *this-is-it* talk.

As he explained to Frank that it would probably be sometime today, they both heard a "no, no!" above them.

As they looked up, there was Virgil, with a long string in his hand, *tying the leaves back on the trees!*

ELEVEN

The Sower of Dreams

If you will let others dream their dreams,
They will share your dreams as well.
If it be business or just seamless seams,
Cheer for them to stand and tell.
Urge them to stand and deliver
Their Great Hope, their soul quiver.
Then it'll be known o'er land and sea
That you are Sower of Dreams
Who sets chained people free!
They will join your great, grand crowd;
Approval will sound, proud and loud.
Then when you tell your dream,
An army will march for your cause
Without doubt, resistance, or pause
To make implausability, plausible
And cause your cause to be causable!

TWELVE

Bunny's Hands

As a pastor for many years, I have heard and seen enough experiences such as I am about to recount that I have become convinced there is something behind them.

Don Harp is a special friend and coworker, whose unabashed honesty is legend around the Palm Beaches.

When I founded Palm Beach Atlantic College and became its first president, it was my job to find an excellent college-level faculty and administrative staff. Without exalting myself, I can say that the good Lord gave us an unbeatable team. Two-thirds of them held Ph.D.s.

Don Harp was close to the top of the list. He was loyal, not a clock-watcher, not abrasive, very kind and courteous. He worked at the college for years, and his retirement banquet was a joy to behold. People came from everywhere to say thanks to Don for his ministry of faithfulness.

A few days after his banquet, I was talking with him about

the death of a mutual friend, when he asked if I minded hearing about the death of his sister, Bunny.

"Say on, Don," I replied.

He recounted that she died at eighteen years of age, when he was just ten.

The family lived in Martinsburg, West Virginia.

Bunny was a gifted musician, singing and playing the piano. She was extremely personable, self-effacing, and greatly talented.

Don adored her. She knew how to relate to a ten-year-old brother.

Quite suddenly, she became ill, and this disturbed young Don. He loved her. He needed her.

When no one has died in one's family, it is quite difficult for a ten-year-old to believe it possible.

They diagnosed it as Hodgkin's.

In the forties, there was no cure for Hodgkin's, even if detected early. Her parents made several trips with her to John's Hopkins in Baltimore. The treatment gave her some temporary relief, but she would soon revert to her increasingly poor state.

She fought to make it to classes in school through her junior year. Six months later, she became bedridden. Terminal was written all over the situation. Terminal!

Young Don was left out of the situation. He acted as most young boys do in a crisis such as this, but he was deeply concerned about Bunny. She was dear to him, dear as life itself.

A sensitive boy of ten can't verbalize, but the seriousness bore deeply into young Don's deepest self. He just stood around, hands in his pockets, looking down and feeling the grimness of the situation.

Don did take care of her when their parents went shopping or to church. This made little Don feel needed, and he was so happy to be of assistance. It helped cover his already covered-deep grief.

She commented that she missed her high school graduation, but she was awaiting an even greater one. Don remembered that.

The final day approached. Bunny could no longer speak, except in short breathy whispers.

One Sunday morning Don and his father were getting dressed for Sunday school. Mother and a friend were staying home with Bunny. Shortly after nine Bunny signaled to her mother, who leaned in to hear.

"I am about to die, Mother."

The tearful family gathered around her bed.

The time was near. *Very near.*

Her eyes opened, staring straight up.

"Listen! Listen!"

Bunny had not been able to move her arms for some time. Both of her arms reached up.

Her eyes filled with absolute wonder. She seemed to be *in touch with something invisible and gloriously beautiful.*

Then her arms fell back. Bunny grew limp. And still.

The passage was complete. The soul released. She had gone to help prepare a future place for Mother, Dad . . . and little Don.

Don Harp is now in his sixties. Both of his parents have also graduated. When he hears some skeptic mocking life after death, he says, "I remember Bunny's dying eyes . . . and uplifted hands."

THIRTEEN

Warren, Missie, and the Boys

Warren and Missie Wahlgren were a find. When I met them, I sensed a special sparkle in everything they did—their walk, conversation, and spirit.

All laughter has a glow, a joy about it; but theirs seemed to have had STP added to it (spirituality, therapy, and personality). Their laughter healed people of depressive attitudes and weak knees.

Did you ever meet someone and know that there was more to their life story than they tell?

The first handshake with Warren relayed a small metal cross into my palm. "Put it in your pocket. Every time you make change and feel that little cross, remember to pray for Warren and Missie!"

The next time I saw him, he handed me a little round piece of wood. It had written on it: "This is a round tuit."

"What is a round tuit?" I asked.

"Every time you procrastinate about doing something important for Christ, remember to get 'around to it.' If you haven't received Christ, get around to it today! If you haven't witnessed to someone, remember now is the time to get around to it. If you haven't given your tithe this week, get around to it."

Often Warren would come to see me at my church office. He never stayed for more than three minutes, but it was fun just to see him come into my study. Warren never came to criticize, scold, or belittle. These words were not in his dictionary. He would have a warm human interest story to tell or some great and sometimes really dumb jokes. His visits were short and sweet.

There was something he wasn't telling me. I made up my mind to get to the bottom of it. One day I said, "Warren, out with it."

"Out with what?"

"That part of your story you haven't told me."

He looked up for a long minute. There are two kinds of minutes: the New York minute, which is as fast as the wind. Then there is the Muleshoe minute, which moves like maple syrup on a cold morning.

If your doctor tells you that you have three months to live, move to Muleshoe, Texas. Those three months will seem like five years.

Warren's upward look was a Muleshoe minute.

When he looked back at me, his eyes were filled with tears.

We have two sons, Rod and Doug. We lived in Sunnyvale, California. There just wasn't anything more wonderful than our family story: a gorgeous wife, two great kids, a great job, a country club membership, and a church we loved.

The boys were great athletes—both champion swimmers. They swam for hours in preparation for coming swim meets.

They had a great swimming coach named Bob Colyer. One day Rod was playing in a championship game. He was the goalie in a water polo match.

We were not at the game that day. Our phone rang. It was Coach Colyer.

"You'd better get here fast. Something has happened to Rod. He collapsed in the pool. We don't know what it is."

When we arrived, the paramedics were there. Missie told me that she would ride in the ambulance, and I could come in the car.

The doctors told us that Rod's heart was quite enlarged, and they didn't know how long he had—a few days at best.

Sixteen-year-old Rod fought hard and long. He fooled them, because he made it through the hospital time, then home. He was paralyzed on one side and had to go through the regimen of the wheelchair, then the walker, then a cane.

He went through four years of the slowest rehabilitation imaginable. By this time he was twenty, and Doug was fourteen.

Now our attention was turned to Doug. Rod's stroke happened when Doug was eleven, and he needed special assurance.

The doctors told Missie that they had better have a look at Doug's heart, "just to make sure."

When the results came from Doug's X rays, their worst fears were confirmed. Same situation, identical malformation of the heart.

This meant that Doug could no longer participate in any athletics. He requested to play just one more game—the big game of the year. He pled with the doctors and us.

The doctors warned us that there might be consequences, but we finally agreed.

"Please, Mom, give me this one gift—just one more game. It's my birthday, Mom. We can cream them. I know we can!"

Missie was at the game. It was a battle to the finish, but it was Doug's fifteenth birthday, and the goalie played as he had never played before.

After a sensational block, the crowd was cheering Doug, when suddenly he collapsed and was floating face down in the pool.

They rushed him to the hospital, where, after everything had been done that could be, Doug died one day into fifteen. Doug had literally played his heart out—on his fifteenth birthday.

This broke our hearts. Our beautiful little fairy-tale family was shattered.

Months went by, and we began to adjust to life without Doug.

We still had Rod. He was a keen kid. We centered ourselves in him, humoring him, letting him know he was special. He, too, was fighting to win, limping around, trying to be helpful at anything anyone would let him.

Of course, we could never forget our little Doug. We talked to Jesus every day and told him to say "Hey!" to Doug. We included him in all our conversations, just as though he were there.

Now we had to concentrate on Rod. He needed something to do around the church, so Pastor Paul gave him a job with the tape ministry. Rod couldn't get enough of it. He loved helping Paul Steele. He loved Paul with all that was left of his heart.

It was Paul who suggested that there be a memorial service for Doug. It was Doug's sixteenth birthday. They scheduled it for the afternoon.

That morning, we were at home, thinking about Doug, and telling Jesus to wish Doug a happy birthday. Rod was at a tape ministry committee meeting and was scheduled to meet us at noon for lunch.

Our phone rang.

"It's Rod," the voice said. "You'd better come quickly."

We drove as fast as we could. When we came into the room, we saw Rod lying on the floor. Rod had gone to meet Doug on his birthday.

A short time later, Pastor Paul called the Wahlgrens.

"I have inoperable prostate cancer. This is great news, because the Lord needs someone to take care of those two before you get there!"

"So, that's the story," Warren said.

"But that isn't the end of it, Warren," I said.

"Why?" Warren asked.

"Because you are going to preach for me Sunday morning and tell that story—just as you've told it to me."

Warren tried to beg off, but I told him that I was the lazy sort, and any time I could take a day off, I would do it.

He told Missie that he couldn't do it.

"You'd better, pal. Someone needs to see a triumphant Christian face death and come out triumphant; and if you don't come out triumphant, I will kick you in the rear!"

I never knew a Christian quite like her.

She made him do it, and we never had a greater service than that fine day in L.A.

A few weeks later Warren got word that his time had come. Cancer. The more rapid sort.

Three days before he died, Warren called me over. I went, and he handed me a letter to the Shepherd of the Hills family. He was already with Rod and Doug before the next week's church paper came out.

WARREN WAHLGREN'S LAST LETTER

(Our lovely friend, Warren Wahlgren, died last Tuesday morning. On Saturday before he graduated from this life, he wrote a letter to the congregation.)

Dear Family,

Oh, you didn't know that sometime back you had been adopted. Well, you are our family, but don't expect us to "pop" for Thanksgiving dinner.

While there is still time, I want to thank everyone for your love, your cards, your gifts, and especially your prayers. They all have been a sustaining force these past months to bolster our faith.

And I won't be able to thank everyone personally here. When we're reunited as a family in God's kingdom, we'll have time to do all these things.

So, brothers and sisters, our kin in Christ, we thank you and say good-bye for a while.

In Love,
Warren Wahlgren

Missie is all alone now—but not really. She is the most humorous, triumphant Christian anyone will ever meet. The neighbors feel the love and joy radiating for blocks around her home in Porter Ranch, just a couple of blocks down the street from the church where Warren preached that day.

FOURTEEN

Warren Wahlgren

His name is Wahlgren.
He made us all grin.
He told us to just do it!
And get around to it.

He put little crosses
In a thousand pockets
And urged us to keep Christ
At the top of our dockets.

He was a dif'rent man than most—
Not given to pride nor to boast.
At the sign of a pain, he'd flash a smile,
And, somehow, ev'rything seemed all worthwhile.

He was man—all man—man all through.
He took life's tasks and held to the true.
To his love, Missie, he says, with a grin,
"You should see the boys—the finest of men!"

"So, we're all up here waiting.
Just Jesus, the boys, and me.
We're happy with joy unabating
Someday, we'll be four, not just three!"

FIFTEEN

The Night God Spoke Out Loud

When I was pastor at First Baptist Church in West Palm Beach, Florida, we were in a building program; and I came up with the idea of building an outdoor worship center on the water. One night at a restaurant—the night before an important building committee meeting—I sketched on the back of a Howard Johnson napkin the idea for the Chapel by the Lake. Later that evening I took it to an artist friend. "I need you to draw this up for me," I said. He was a little taken aback by my coming to him so late, but he was a good friend, so he said, "Sure. When do you need it?"

"Tomorrow," I said. He gasped, yelled at me a little bit, and said OK. The next morning I took the plans to the deacons. And we built it! It had a pulpit shaped like the prow of a boat, and people came by boat and yacht to worship at this chapel on the intercoastal canal. It was a beautiful little place—still is.

One night I needed a place to hide out and write an article, so I went to the chapel. I decided to write in the control booth, since it was secluded and quiet. I became engrossed in the writing process, so I didn't hear anyone come in. But suddenly I heard two boys talking loudly, laughing and cursing.

One of them said to the other, "Why don't you go up into the pulpit where that blankety-blank Moody preaches and get those blankety-blank deacons to take up an offering and bring you the money so you can buy a new car."

I was horrified, to say the least, and wondered what in the world I was going to do. They didn't know I was there, and I wasn't keen on coming out of the sound booth, but I didn't want them hanging around.

Suddenly the Lord sent a little angel to whisper in my ear, "You're in the control booth, Moody!" My mind began to whirl with the possibilities. Before I knew it, I had turned on the sound, full blast, and put the mike almost in my mouth.

As those boys stood on the stage, pretending to preach (while cursing like sailors) in our beautiful chapel, I boomed at them through the sound system, "I am the Lord your God, who led you out of Egypt! You shall have no other gods before me!"

You should have seen their faces. They tucked their tails and ran, and all I saw were two shirttails flying around the corner of the building.

Those boys are now on the mission field, having heard the call of God in the night. (Not really. They're probably in the penitentiary. But it makes a great ending!)

SIXTEEN

A Biblical Fun Puzzle

The names of 16 books of the Bible are mentioned in the paragraph below. See how many you can find. (A minister found 15 books in 20 minutes. But it took him weeks to find the sixteenth one. Let's see how much time it takes you.)

I once made a remark about the hidden books of the Bible. It was a lulu; kept people looking so hard for facts . . . and for others it was a revelation. Some were in a jam, especially since the names of the books were not capitalized. But the truth finally struck home to numbers of our readers. To others it was a real job. We want it to be a most fascinating few moments for you. Yes, there will be some really easy ones to spot. Others may require judges to help them. I will quickly admit it usually takes a minister to find one of them, and there will be loud lamentations when it is found.

A little lady says she brews a cup of tea so she can concentrate better. See how well you can compete. Relax now, for there really are sixteen names of books of the Bible in this paragraph.

SEVENTEEN

The Agoraphobic Academy Award Winner

Al Kasha's name is legend in Hollywood. But he was deep-six sick.

Nominated four times and two times winner of the Oscar. Fame, money, family—everything . . . but hope. It was just a town in Arkansas, not a psychological characteristic for Al.

Hope had fled in the night amidst flashing cameras; TV interviews; autographs; royalty checks; faithful wife, Ceil; and a beautiful daughter who loved him.

There was night in the night of his soul at night. There was night in his soul at high noon light. Someone or something had taken the color out of the palette of his psyche.

His emotional color range went from gray to black.

It was over. Suicidal thoughts had killed his creativity—and almost made him unemployable.

Enter one Bob Munger. A strange, blunt man, who had just

produced a movie called *Born Again* about the Watergate hatchet man, Charles Colson.

Munger came to see Al. He was there on a mission—to share his personal faith in Jesus Christ. He said he witnessed because every time he did, his faith grew.

Bob had heard that Al was swimming in Lake Blue Funk, with fainting spells, hyperventilation, heart palpitations, and an overwhelming urge to hide. He could not face the outside world. He couldn't drive, or carry on a good conversation.

Munger shared his faith with Al, a Jewish boy from the Bronx, whose father made a punching bag of him, whose paranoiac mother greatly preferred the other brother, Larry, who was a successful producer.

"My mother was the East Coast distributor of guilt," Al said later. Al was the laboratory where she conducted the perfection of the guilt before she distributed it.

This resulted in Al's psyche being mix-mastered into the emotional mush he had become.

He kept his room in semidarkness. He didn't answer phone calls or meet people. When the meter man came to the house, Al would hide until the meter reader was gone.

This went on for weeks.

It would be unthinkable that he could ever face the insanity of the Los Angeles freeway, the "I love you, dahling!" kissy-kissy Hollywood mock love, and the "Let's do lunch someday" routine.

The one good result of his sickness was that it cured him of the absolute phoniness, the script-pushing, part-seeking, character-assassinating, wire-pulling rat maze that most

Americans think is the *ultima, the ultimate rush, the radical most* of fame and fortune.

Al now saw it for the garbage that it is—and he had been cured of ever believing that this is what is important in his life. Something else had to come in, and this good, broken man was facing either death or eternal life.

Finally, one day he came to the wall that all the children of the fall come to: now or never, forward to life or backward to death!

His Rubicon!

He knelt down and confessed his darkness to Christ and asked for forgiveness and cleansing.

The deep, deep cleansing came.

Al's heart became the Golden Gate through which Jesus entered astride the little donkey of humility.

The King had entered!

Al Kasha, the Academy Award winner, now lay the Oscars as palm fronds for the triumphal entry to take place.

He felt the hate, the phoniness, the utter stupidity of fame-seeking, and money-grabbing *roaring* out of every pore in his body.

He was clean, every whit of him, every bit of him.

At one moment he could not leave his home. At this crystal moment he could not stay in the house.

He felt like rocking and rolling right down the middle of the freeway!

I met him shortly after that. We became fast friends. I baptized him, ordained him to the ministry, loved him and adored the Kashas as few people I know.

He taught a Sunday school class for actors, the "Act-One" in the Shepherd of the Hills. Now he teaches hundreds of actors, writers, producers, directors—as well as best boys, wire pullers, grips, and wanna-be's from all over the acting world.

Don't tell Al Kasha that Jesus Christ is not real.

He'll smile you right out of your argument.

EIGHTEEN

Karl

It was winter. I mean the shuddery, why-did-I-ever-leave-home-this-morning kind of day, the sort of day that freezes your teeth together, where saliva leaves the mouth in liquid and arrives on the ground as ice. My feet were screaming for warmth and threatening to turn ice blue.

We were in Norway. Winter of '47. Check it out. One of the coldest in a decade. If I had been scheduled to preach that day, hell would have been a welcome subject.

Bob Randall, my teammate on a preaching mission for Youth for Christ and the world's most loyal friend, would have been loyal only to a warm brick that morning.

We were going to church at the Ansgar Church in Bergen. I was surprised that the place wasn't packed because it was a toasty, welcome-home kind of feel when we entered and were greeted by Dr. Gordon Johnson, a physician, patriot, and great Christian leader.

"Texans having a problem with our inhospitable weather. It is a little chilly outside!"

We guffawed at his very perverted sense of humor.

Once the morning service began, I realized how very warm a church service could be. It was one of the grand experiences of my life.

The people had just come out of the rigors of WWII. They knew the thrill of freedom of worship. They were happy in Christ. They had been overrun by the Nazis. Now they were free indeed!

Peace is when sons bury their fathers. War is when fathers bury their sons. Old faces that buried their sons know how to worship the living Christ.

Every choir member had a guitar, from large bass to little ukelike mandolins. They sang a song America had not heard at that time, "How Great Thou Art." If I had been smart, I would have done what another enterprising American was wise enough to do—copyright it and introduce it to the Christians in the United States.

To hear the roar of glory, fifty stringed instruments and fifty voices of freedom-worshiping saints will cause the bells of total joy to be released in one's soul. It was enough to make an Episcopal bishop dance in the aisles!

Dr. Johnson's father, Gustav ("Call me Gus"), whom I assume was a retired minister, stood up and welcomed us to the Norwegian fellowship of happy believers.

He was speaking Norwegian, which we did not understand, and he suddenly broke into perfect English: "Aim high! Keep shy! and Draw nigh! Take that back to America and preach it!"

I have preached that to young people all over America . . . for fifty years.

Pastor Riese, a tall, courtly gentleman, with a resonance in his voice that shivered the timbers of that old church, exhalted the living King Jesus. What a glorious memory-sticker it was!

After the service, we all went to the Ansgar Hotel for Sunday dinner. Bob and I were babbling compliments to them and enjoying the sumptuous food.

We had just come from Britain where rationing was still quite severe. I had lost thirty-six pounds in a very few months, and good food was welcomed with gustatorial ecstasy. We munched with such gladness that I am afraid we were an embarrassment to the hosts. Actually, they seemed to enjoy our enjoyment of the finest cooking of the Norwegian mothers, who seemed gleeful that we were such enthusiastic smackers, yummy-ers, and wow-ers over their delightful preparations.

After the meal Dr. Johnson stood at the table, raised a toast, and said simply, "To Karl." They all stood and shouted, "To Karl!"

We didn't understand what it meant. I am not certain what it meant, even today. It was a toast to a young lad from one of their families, whose story is quite amazing.

The Nazis had taken over Norway, with all the meaning that that phrase conjures in one's mind.

There was a Norwegian lad named Karl, who was commandeered by the Nazis to drive a bus for the officers of the Third Reich. For weeks Karl drove them from one meeting place to another. He was a quiet lad, perhaps nineteen years old.

The Germans used the Norwegian hills as a rendevous place for some major planning of the war down in Western Europe. On a certain day there was something special in the air. Karl sensed it when he noted that several major officers from the front were flown into Bergen—about thirty of them.

Karl was to drive them to their high-mountain Eagle's Nest meeting place. It was a serious drive, involving negotiating high mountain curves. Another truck was following them.

There was laughter and jesting among the officers, as the bus wended its way out of Bergen, en route to the Eagle's Nest.

Karl was a careful driver, who had gained their confidence by faithfully executing what he was supposed to do—drive the countryside that he knew like the back of his hand. That day Karl had negotiated the bus to the high mountains. They were less than a few hundred feet from their destination, coming around a sharp curve on a high peak. Suddenly Karl turned the steering wheel sharply to the right, plunging the bus, filled with screaming Nazi officers, off a twenty-five-hundred-foot cliff. He did it for freedom.

Tears coursed down our cheeks as we listened to the story of Karl's incredible sacrifice. My friend, Bob, leaped to his feet, raised his water glass upward and shouted: "To Karl!"

We all stood and said once again, more loudly: "To Karl!"

NINETEEN

The Truchas Night Rider

Truchas is a town in New Mexico, but it is more. I dare you to go there, sit in silence for an hour, and not be haunted by the fact that the streets whisper "story, story, story!"

My longtime friend, Bill Tate, now deceased, loved to tell me Truchas stories. His best, I think, was that when someone died, the Truchas night visitor, a horseman, would ride slowly through the streets, from house to house. Past midnight an old man on horseback would ride up to a home and with a long stick, would waken the house and announce that one of the townspeople had died.

"Juan Martin está muerto."

From inside the house the people answer, "Juan Martin no está muerto."

Old man: "I see no evidence that Juan Martin is not dead. Why is he not dead?"

They answer: "Because Jesus said, 'I am the resurrection

and the life. He that believeth on me, though he were dead, yet shall he live.'"

The old man then asks, "Where is the light of faith in your house?"

Lights come on all over the house. The little town would become ablaze with the lights of faith. Then the people come out of their houses and start dancing in the streets.

This is repeated until the streets are filled with dancing people, celebrating the fact that Juan Martin no está muerto! The Resurrection Dance.

The town is ablaze with faith! Because "Juan Martin no está muerto!"

TWENTY

Schaller and Moody at the Bobcat Bite

Lyle Schaller was speaking at the North American Baptist Missions Conference at Glorieta, New Mexico. His plain midwestern, whimsical, no-nonsense approach blessed us all with the keenest insights I had heard in years.

After one of the meetings, I introduced myself.

He said, "Let's have lunch."

Thank God, he didn't say, "Let's do lunch." California style. The very phrase smacks of such gross phoniness and California kissy-kissy, which indicates that our society has reached the point that we need a daytime serial called "As the Stomach Turns."

To me Lyle Schaller was a legend. His books had permeated the world with incisive analysis and extreme wisdom, until even the secularists consulted him.

To preachers, as I said, Schaller is a legend.

"How about a no-ambience mountain dump of a place

that has people clammering to get in? It's called the Bobcat Bite."

"Game!" he said.

As we drove to the Bite, I told him that the *L.A. Times* carried a great article about the place. It said that the only way to get a seat there at noon would be for one of the regulars to die.

As we sat munching a huge five-star hamburger, sitting at the counter—all other seats were taken—I relished the Schallerisms.

"We must understand that the great preachers of today will be off the scene as we face 2020. The man who will lead us is now a twelve-year-old boy in Evansville, Indiana." Using that image as a sort of Middletown, USA model.

"The most money should be spent by the denominations, right now, on reaching the junior-high kids."

Then he stoked my already flaming attention.

"'We are losing our kids,' said a sociologist, who—of all things—is an atheist. 'The only hope is our churches!'"

He didn't document the source because that would be a heck of a complex way to converse. Imagine someone punctuating his conversation with a bunch of *ibids.*

Schaller continued: "We must have thousands of preachers to come from this present culture. You had plenty coming from the South, but that was when it was a culture of belief. Now you must get them from the South and the rest of the nation as well. The rest of the nation is a culture of unbelief, and the South is rapidly becoming the same."

His words staggered me. I thought, *Could it be that the Southern Spiritual Udder is going dry?*

Schaller marched on: "And, to repeat, you must start with the twelve-year-olds."

Half of my hamburger lay there, and anything that can coax me away from a Bobcat Bite hamburger is some electronic magnet!

Schaller was that magnet.

I injected the question, "Do you know the Lutheran pastor, Walt Kallestat?"

"Yes, from Phoenix—great guy!" Schaller beamed.

"I hear he's trying to do something about that, with a massive emphasis on children."

"Well, if that's what he is doing, he's on the right track."

"Can we carry that logic, about reaching the twelve-year-olds, a bit further?" I asked.

"Yes, let those kids know that you believe in them, and that you need their advice. They know far more about their world than the scholars. Give your best twelve-year-olds a ministaff position."

"A ministaff position?" I injected.

"Sure, Put a mentor over each ministaff member. Make sure the mentors have decent training about what they are doing. Maybe a staff member could do it. College is far too late."

I had to speak. "Man, that last word rings a bell in my heart. It seems that so many colleges, at least in my denomination, are trying to start graduate schools."

"Too late!" Schaller responded, "Far too late!"

He was emphatic about it.

I thought of a program at the college I founded, Palm

Beach Atlantic College, where—during the summer—high schoolers are brought in for a sampling of college life.

I felt I could hear Schaller's answer to that idea: "Too late!"

Then I thought of the program at our Baptist assemblies, Glorieta and Ridgecrest, called Centrifuge, where the twelve-and-ups are given a rigorous but totally fun time, replete with Christian mentors, Bible teaching, inspirational and commitment times, and just plain kid stuff.

"That's great, but not enough."

I remember, at First, Van Nuys, California, we had a summer youth program, called SuperSummer, for teenagers.

The ghost of Schaller will always haunt me with his "too late!"

"Our number one issue today is leadership. College is too late."

A direct Schaller quote.

My mind whirled out a few embryonics. Why not?

Why not call a meeting of some of the brightest twelve-year-olds and really get into their lives until we find their thoughts, their desires, and their dreams. Getting past athletics, and the fragile, surface stuff; and really digging until we strike the gold of their essential essence—and really put Christ into them *before* adolescence.

Why not?

Denominations, for the most part, have some pretty worn-out programs, or they are too narrow in their targeting, emphasizing only one theme, for the twelve-year-old of today.

To invite them to study, as an example, *missions,* great as it is, is not enough. They are facing, in the next very few months, powerful minicomputers—cell phones in their back-packs on which they can access the entire world while waiting for the school bus. They need to sophisticate their response mechanism to what they face on the Net. Cults lurk, porno possesses, pagans philosophize sterile scholarship, and the idiot-rantings of one-lung intellectuals seek them.

Instead of getting into the battle, Christians have tradition-ally fought with intellectual swords for a season, then given up and set up an evangelical counter movement on a small island, and watched the big ships go by, captained by government sponsored, secularly trained, mentally neutered, intellectual ventriloquist dummies, mouthing John Dewey's shibboleths. We will never get out on the high seas when we keep our ships in port. Christians are made to steer, not simply watch.

But, on the more hopeful side, the secularists are discover-ing that Schaller's atheist friend is right. "The only hope we have is in the churches."

We must merit the appellation and train our twelve-year-olds for future captaining. But a lot of them are being washed overboard.

They won't go overboard if they are taught . . . that their mind is God's gift and belongs *only* to them . . . that they are not little computer cards with thirty-five numbers on them . . . that they didn't come from some backwater swamp, the prod-uct of zero-IQ cells, instead of being the high-born children of God that they are.

Get *that* lodged in a twelve-year-old brain, and he will be like the first-century Christians who "turned the world upside down."

Actually, those early Christians didn't turn the world upside down—they turned it right-side-up. It had already been turned upside down by sin.

Lyle Schaller knows how to interpret that upside, downside world.

And he wants the twelve-year-olds to repeat that early first-century trick and turn the upside down, right side up!

TWENTY-ONE

I Found a Son for Burt Reynolds

Burt cohosted the *Mike Douglas Show* and asked that I be on it with him. That week Todie Fields, Mel Tillis, Tony Orlando, and a dozen other celebrity types appeared with us.

As far as I am concerned, the hit of the week was Jim, Burt's adopted brother and football coach at Forest Hill High School in West Palm Beach. He was the coach of our son, Pat, and was a profoundly good influence on him. Jim is naturally funny. He almost upstaged Burt.

When Burt asked Jim how the team looked this year, he replied, "Oh, they look good, good. We have over a hundred boys out for the team. The only problem is that you can take the whole team, coaches and all, in three Volkswagens!

"We had our first game last week, and we did pretty good. Listen, those kids really pulled together. You can do a lot of things if you have teamwork. Why, we made a first down in the first half—and, and it was *against the wind.*"

"We made another one in the second half—and that one was in *tall grass!*"

Jim goes on like that all the time.

One bit of conversation during the show revealed Burt's wild interest in having a little boy. (The good Lord later gave him one, Quinton, whom we dedicated in our church, with Ricardo Montalban and his lovely wife, who is Loretta Young's sister, acting as the sponsors.)

I was really taken aback the next week when at least a score of women volunteered to be the mother, if Burt so desired.

I knew America's moral standards were low . . . but . . . !

Burt wanted, was aching deeply, to have a boy.

It wasn't show-biz talk to drum up interest or increase his popularity. He *really* wanted a child.

Later that week, Burt sang (and quite well) a song written by Dick Feller, "Room for a Boy . . . Never Used."

He tore that sucker out and stomped it flat, as Ray Blount said. That tugged at the hearts of millions of American women.

How do I know that? Because two tons and a brick load of women called me, wrote me, came to me, begged me, threatened me if I didn't arrange for Burt to see their child, sire their child, rent their child, or whatever.

I didn't have time to prepare a sermon, eat lunch, or go to the bathroom because there was always some woman grabbing me, telling me that God had revealed unto her in the night—that God's love would overlook the indiscretion for this child to be born. (None of them called it adultery, which is what God says it is!) It was unreal!

It was then that I got an idea that would solve this problem. I went to a Seminole Indian leader (I can't recall his name) to ask for a child for Burt. *After all,* my brilliant mind raced, *wasn't Burt part Indian, and hadn't he played football for the Florida State Seminoles?*

The Indian people would be proud and honored to have a famous, wealthy movie actor become the adoptive father of one of theirs. The Seminoles would love it! I had it all worked out.

The Seminoles were not in the least impressed by my naive pitch.

"Seminoles don't have orphans. It is the duty of the whole tribe to care for Seminole children whose parents have died."

The Indian leader, whom I will call "Billy" after Billy Bowlegs, the great Seminole leader, wasn't remotely interested in my proposition.

"Besides, do you think for one minute that we would allow one of our precious little children to be exposed to the white American value system? We are mainly Christians.

"Most of us are Baptists. You are a Baptist Christian; we are Christian Baptists. You are a part of the white person's value system. Your value system comes from your culture, and you superimpose it over your Christianity.

"We were pagans, with a pagan value system. Christ was brought to us by Baptist missionaries. We accepted Christ, and that meant the elimination of the old way of thinking—not an accommodation.

"We don't need big-name movie stars to augment our weak egos, to make us feel like we are somebody. We are already somebody in Christ!"

"But . . . but Burt is part Indian," I countered. "He would study your ways, your customs, and learn to abide by them.

"Also, I am part Cherokee. . . ."

I was getting in deeper than I had ever intended. I felt outdone, outwitted, outmoraled, and out-Christianed! How did I know Burt would study their customs, learn them, and abide by them. I couldn't speak for Burt. I got back to my only point in the case.

"Anyway," as I said, "Burt is part Indian."

"And he is part *white!*"

Billy closed the case and locked the door.

I have never told Burt this story, and he will only know it when he reads it here. I pray that this experience will bring Burt and Jess to look a little more deeply into our Indian and Christian heritage.

We must all come to the conclusion that we don't want to be Baptist (or Methodist or Presbyterian) Christians, but Christian Baptists, with our priorities centered on seeking *first* the kingdom of God, and his righteousness. We must not be seeking *first* the present sick, secular system, so selectively serialized by Satan himself.

Meanwhile, every conversation I had with Burt, he would bring up what Jim, his brother, called "The Kid Bit."

It was at that time that our church purchased a psychiatrist's clinic next door to the church. It was owned by a child psychiatrist. Through my contact with this situation, I found the child for my friend.

While walking through the building, I found the most magnificently stuffed chimpanzee one could ever hope to see.

"At last, I have found the answer to the 'Kid Bit.'"

I called Jim and told him that I had just the child for "the Star."

"But Jess, what do you know about his parents?"

"Very similar."

I hoped that Big Burt, Burt's dad, would forgive me.

"I'll be right over; but I can tell you right now that, though he is crazy to make this happen, Burt will be very cautious about this kid."

When Jim arrived, filled with apprehension, I immediately introduced him to "Burt the third."

Jim loved it.

"Maybe this will relieve the tension that has been mounting about this thing. Let's do it!"

I called Burt.

"Your worries are over! I have a child for you. He is beautiful, has an IQ about your level, and you will be totally surprised about how much he looks like you."

I should be defrocked.

"Whoa, Jess, Whoa! I don't know anything about him. His parents. His pedigree. His total background check. I must know all before I take a step this serious."

His staccato speech made me know that I had the Star in the hollow of my grimy hands!

"Look, Buddy, it's too late," I said, using Burt's nickname. I have already done everything, made all the arrangements. Everything. He is already signed over to you. . . . I took the liberty of signing in your behalf."

"You *what!!!???*"

He used a few unprintables at this point. Actually, he was using the same words I use in the pulpit on Sunday morning. The arrangement and aim of them are only slightly altered.

"Now, Buddy, I know you are a little upset."

"A *little!!!???*"

"But I have already signed the papers. Hold on just a moment. Jim has just arrived. He'll tell you it's all OK."

I was sitting on the floor, laughing my gizzard out, cupping the phone. I signaled Jim over to me. There I sat with this large, stuffed monkey jammed into my mouth to silence my screams. The monkey and I were both shaking from head to toe.

Jim sized up the situation and straight-faced right into the conversation:

"Buddy, Moody has already scored a ninety-eight-yard run for you. It is a six-pointer in the last three seconds of the game."

"Jim, I want Moody tracked down, tied down. He is a loose cannon. I have never . . . and he calls himself my friend!"

He was rabid.

"Buddy, don't talk stupid. *Reverend* Moody has stood tall for you. You told the whole nation that you wanted a boy. *You* sang 'Room for a Boy . . . Never Used.' Everyone will be thrilled for you. It will be the talk of the world."

"I don't care if the kid is Thomas Alva Edison, Jonas Salk, or St. Francis of Assisi! I don't want *anybody* giving me a child if I haven't checked him out!"

Then, in a voice, filled with fear and insecurity, he said, "Jim, buddy, is it too late?"

Jim then sounded like Digger O'Dell, in his most funereal voice: "It's too late, Buddy, the baby is yours."

"I'm calling my lawyer right now. That Jess Moody will be sorry he was ever born. I'll nail him to the wall."

"They did that to Jess's Boss, and it didn't work. Now let me lay it on the line, Burt . . . The kid is all alone. He . . . he was *abandoned.* They found him in a closet, danged closet, Burt. They don't even know who his parents are!"

I could have kissed Jim. *If Burt could act like that,* I thought, *he would have won the Oscar a long time ago.*

"What???!!! You don't even know who his parents are? That's worse! They found him . . . in a closet . . . and they don't even know who his parents are . . . this kid might have some kind of incurable disease. Maybe his parents left him because of something like that!"

"Buddy, you are talking crazy. Now, cool off. This little boy is precious."

That did it for me. I stuffed that monkey halfway down my throat when Jim said "precious."

Somehow Jim and "precious" just don't seem to belong together.

"Bud, I'm bringing him over right now. Now that's all there is to it. You run and get some diapers, baby wipes, some baby bottles. Don't forget the nipples."

"Diapers. Wipes! This is crazy. O, God, I'm going to have this baby, screaming, screaming his little head off, I don't know how to take care of . . . Diapers and wipes! Help me! What size do I get?"

Mr. Calm said, "Six and seven-eighths diaper, and size C

wipes. He's got a pretty big rear end, and it's kinda' *red*. He'll need good, long-term care.

"Anyway, Bud, I'm on my way. You'll go crazy with love when you see him. He's the cutest little dark-complexioned kid you'll ever see."

"Wait, Jim, wait. Don't hang up. Wait!"

Jim hung up.

See Jim fall on the floor.

See Jim holding his sides!

See Jim totally out of control!

"Six-and-seven-eighths diaper and size C wipes! You are a genius, Jim, a sheer genius! Six-and-seven-eighths diaper! Where did you get *that?*"

The tears were rolling off my chin.

"Well, his head looked to be about the same size as his rear. I figured he'd wear about a six-and-seven-eighths hat, so . . ."

Jim put the monkey back in the car, buckled him in, got in the driver's seat, and roared away.

Meanwhile, back at the ranch, the star of stage and screen was pitching a conniption fit that outconniptioned any conniption ever conniptioned.

"When Jim drives up with that kid, I won't go out there. No six-and-seven eighths diaper—nothing!"

When Jim drove up to the ranch house in Jupiter, the place was totally quiet. He found Buddy in a back room, sunk deep down in a huge chair. His head barely showed over the armrests.

"I'll kill you. You'll never get me out to that car!"

"Now, Bud . . . now, now, Bud."

"Don't now, now, Bud me!"

"His little eyes are popping out of their sockets. . . . He is sooo excited about his new daddy, Burt! Look, if you don't love him when you see him, I'll take him."

"Yeah! Jo, Jamie Jo, and Buddy—they'll love that. Bringing home a little naked baby—how are you going to explain *that* to Jo?"

"I'll get Jess to explain all about how he had to go to so much trouble to sign off for this child, and how coldly you turned him down."

Then Jim master-stroked.

"I can see it in the *National Enquirer* now, Bud, at thousands of checkout lines all over America: BURT REYNOLDS COLDLY TURNS ORPHAN BABY AWAY!"

"Oh, NO!"

Like a prisoner, walking the last mile, Burt trudged out, shoulders down.

"Let's go, Jim."

He walked toward the car at the slowest pace imaginable. Finally, he looked in. He saw this stuffed chimp, staring out at him.

"O Yes! Yes! Yes! I want him!"

He took the newly adopted child and danced all over the front yard with him.

A few nights later Doris and I were the guests of Burt, Burt Sr., and Fern for dinner.

There, in a little director's chair, right in the center of the den, sat the monkey, looking right at us, with a little sign around his neck, "Jess, Jr."

And pinned on him was a diaper—size six-and-seven-eighths!

TWENTY-TWO

Raising Beaver Cleaver Kids in a Beavis and Butthead World

I was pastor of a large church in what is now the second largest city in the United States, Los Angeles.

And I am deeply troubled about the educational system.

The obvious aside, I am also concerned about the dreadful lack of desire on the part of the average young person to want to go to college.

Almost never do I hear a high school graduate say anything other than that he/she is going to get a job, look around for something better, maybe try to make it in "the business" (code word for the motion picture industry), and if that doesn't work, maybe be a salesman. ("I have a friend who makes pretty good money selling bottled water, driving a delivery truck.") But that comes later.

Here is a kid who can barely put sentences together, can't spell *cain't,* and is absolutely doomed to mediocrity or below, simply because school, church, parents, peer group, and society in general don't create any conscience about being ready for the fierce welter of mass nihilism that is mashing the bejabbers out of the minds of our kids.

One thing that displeases me about our children is that they think very little about going above high school.

Live in a smaller house, drive economy cars, get your clothes at Wal-Mart, or the Price Club, so you can save money—lots of it—for your child's education.

It is the ultimate profanity not to make up your mind that your child will have drilled, drummed, and concretized in his/her brain that college and graduate work is a must, an absolute must, period, case closed!

You say, "I didn't get very much education, and I did OK."

That we are in a time of radical time compression, ego-crushing, enthroning of hedonism, and nihilism is not a subject of debate. Everybody knows subconsciously that something in the air is terribly amiss, and far be it from me to try to interpret this. But I know enough to warn parents that good, solid, serious commitment to a morally based education must be every parent's greatest commitment.

The Beaver Cleavers are running this country, and the Beaver Cleavers will run it in the next generation and every generation that will ever come. The Beavis-Buttheads will work for them, at about a fourth of the salaries the much maligned Beaver Cleavers will make. It is as irreversible as gravity. You can't do away with a sunrise just because it is your choice to sit in darkness.

The first time Willy Lump-Lump tells you that he's not going to college, hoist him to a pittard, threaten him with a long stroll on a short gangplank, put him in irons down in the hold for thirty days, make him never forget the transgression. And tell the society that is coddling him and criticizing you for standing up to your kid's apathy, "This is my son or daughter—and you leave him alone."

Your child will either be a Generation X child (Xed out!), or he will be a Generation O child (Opportunity!). The choice isn't his/hers—it is yours to make.

I dare you to wade through the next long sentence and reread it three times. My parents faced two burn-outs of their café businesses, a major depression, cancer, tuberculosis, triple major surgeries, no welfare, a tiny Social Security check, and, by the grace of God, plus guts-you-wouldn't-believe, they saw to it that I earned two major degrees, plus Oxford, plus several honorary degrees thrown in!

Horace and Connie Moody: he, with a third-grade education, and she, with a tenth-grade education, so planted a lust for the learning they were never able to have, that I founded Palm Beach Atlantic College, now a university, one of the best colleges on the east coast of Florida.

Dizzy Dean was right: "It ain't bragging if it's so!"

My mother sold her Christmas gift watch to give me the first money I took with me to go to Baylor University. Her dresses went out of style because she made the old ones do for one more year. Some people may have looked down on her because she wasn't "in." She was "out of it" so I could be "in on it."

Her old dresses were badges of honor. Costumes of Christ!

My dad pried the baseboard off the kitchen floor, where he

put some few coins "for a rainy day" to help pay my dorm rent.

You know why they were doing this, don't you? They knew what it was like to be left out, not chosen, put down because they didn't have the education to step up a little higher on the ladder of financial and social success. And by the grace of God and the grace of guts, they weren't going to let that happen to me! And it didn't.

Every time I have been "robed," while receiving an honorary doctorate, I have tearfully said under my breath: "Thanks Horace and Connie for prying the baseboard loose and selling the Christmas gift watch!"

When I stood up to deliver the baccalaureate address at the Air Force Academy, I publicly thanked Horace and Connie, which I called the "H and C Corporation," for putting me there.

When I spoke at the White House and wrote President Ford's address before the Southern Baptist Convention at Norfolk, Virginia, I whispered, "Thanks H and C Corporation."

When I have stood at conventions, conclaves, conferences, and university chapels, I have stood in the name of Jesus Christ and the H and C Corporation, a major watch and baseboard company.

God knows I am not bragging about my accomplishments; I am praising this unknown and little regarded twosome, whose bodies have lain in a small plot in an old graveyard in San Angelo, Texas, for thirty years.

I am more honored by them than when I attended the royal wedding of Princess Elizabeth and Phillip Mountbatten.

As a matter of fact, I was sent there by the H and C Corporation to represent the King of kings.

The same great tribute could be paid to my Doris's parents, Fletcher and Jessie Cummins. He was a leather craftsman, and she went door-to-door selling cemetery plots. Their income was meager; their riches in Christ major.

They gave me the best wife a man could ever want, sent her to Baylor University, where God brought us together. They saw to the education of both of their daughters, Doris and Joyce. I couldn't have made it without the F and J Company insisting that their children receive the best, while they "made do" with the least.

I am quite certain that not enough credit is given to parents who pay the price, the tremendous price, of educating their kids.

Dad, step up to the plate. If you have to make a choice between a Beemer or a good used Ford, make it; and your grateful kid will rise up and maybe buy you a Rolls!

Mother, make those clothes do, and live in a smaller house, and see that your children learn how to do those things that will make the difference.

Someday, One will robe you better than anything Paris can concoct, and give you a house not made with hands, where there won't be too much month at the end of the money and the air-conditioning won't go out!

TWENTY-THREE

A Top Priority
Church Member

1. I will go to church to sow happy thoughts, friendliness, and the tithe of the harvest of my earnings.
2. As I drive to my church, I will increase my eagerness to worship with each block nearer to our worship place.
3. I will say something exciting about my church as I enter the parking lot.
4. I will say, "Hi, God's house! Surprise me today!"
5. As I enter the building, I will smile at the usher and say to his face, "Thank you for being a welcome sign for God."
6. I will look around and smile at the people—especially those I don't know.
7. I will say, "Every person here is a good friend of my best friend, Jesus, so they are potentially good friends of mine!"

8. I will say something good about the pastor. The only currency he has to spend is his good reputation. If anyone says anything to diminish that, I will stand up for the pastor, no matter how embarrassing it may be. A reputation thief is worse than a thief of money.

9. I will say good things about the music and educational leaders, their assistants, and their programs. A good church cannot exist without them.

10. I will sing with joy as I hear music put to the world's greatest thoughts.

11. I will take notes on my pastor's sermon. He spends a lot of time praying and preparing it.

12. I will consider the sermon to be a baton, something to hand off to someone else in the race.

13. I will tell the pastor what I liked most about his message.

14. I will write the pastor a warm, loving, noncritical letter at least once a year.

15. As I leave the place, I will shake hands with seven people, tell them what a great service it was, and say, "Don't we have a wonderful church with wonderful people in it! If you haven't joined, I hope you will. We need good people like you here!"

16. I will have a little card printed saying, "You encouraged me by being in church today. Thank you!"

TWENTY-FOUR

The Stranger in the Foggy Night

I was out for a near dawn walk.

Across from Golden Gate Seminary, it was impossible to see the San Francisco skyline. I heard the monotonous low moan of fog-warning signals from what few ships were out in a morning like this.

An old joke I told while preaching in London, years ago, came to my mind.

"Mo'ning Jock."

"Mo'ning John."

"Ever seen the fog any thicker?"

"Only once."

"'n where was that?"

"Dunno, the fog was too thick to tell!"

Bad joke for Americans. Goes over well in London, where they know what real fog is.

But there was something quite wonderful about that

splendid isolation I was experiencing in my morning walk on the Golden Gate Bridge.

God thoughts. Splendid isolation. I always connect my devotions with some activity. Example: Every step up the stairs has a name of someone for whom I pray as I climb. The light switch reminds me that Christ is the light of the world. Salt at breakfast reminds me to be salt that day.

O, I am a wonderfully spiritual man, I am! More than most, I congratulate myself.

I was consumed with the spiritual as well as the spiritual energy that was surging through me. The chilling dawn only added to the zest of my very spiritual quest.

Suddenly, I was frightened by a shout from some invisible source out there in the foggy bank.

"I'm going to do it, so help me, I am!"

I walked in the direction of the sound. Suddenly, facing me was a man, his face contorted with a terrible anxiety of some sort. He was hanging off the outside bridge railing. Just the release of his grip and he would fall hundreds of feet into San Francisco Bay.

"Oh, please don't do that!" I begged.

"I'm going to do it. Nothing can stop me. Life is too terrible. No one cares for me!"

My marvelous spiritual insight indicated that in his last quote there was a way.

"I know someone who loves you deeply. His name is Jesus Christ."

"I am a Christian," he responded.

"Good! What is your church?"

"Baptist."

"Great! So am I!" More identification. *We're getting somewhere,* I thought.

"Are you American Baptist, Conservative Baptist, North American Baptist, or Southern Baptist?"

"Southern Baptist."

"Wonderful! Are you a California Southern Baptist?"

"Yes."

Now we're getting somewhere. It won't be long until he is off that railing.

I was feeling good about my great counseling skills.

"Are you a member of a Southern Baptist Association?"

"Yes, the San Francisco Bay Association."

"Why, I'm speaking there, tonight. Do you believe Jesus is the Savior of the world?"

"Yes, I do."

"Do you believe he was as much man as if he were not God at all?"

"Yes."

"And that he was as much God as if he were not man at all?"

"Yes."

"That he had two minds, two wills, two natures?"

"Yes, yes I do."

He's beginning to get hope, I thought. *Jess Moody, you are so good at this!* I congratulated myself.

"And do you believe in the hypostatic union of the natures of Jesus?"

"Yes, I do."

"Do you believe in the richochet of the eschata?"

"Yes, as a matter of fact, I came to understand that only yesterday."

"Wonderful!" My brillant mind was racing.

"Do you believe in limited, or unlimited atonement?"

"Unlimited."

I shoved him off the bridge.

"Die, you despicable heretic!"

And I continued jogging into the dense fog . . .

TWENTY-FIVE

Hard Evidence for the Resurrection

THE COURTROOM EVIDENCE

1. 643 eyewitnesses from the New Testament.
2. More than 2,000,000,000 accepted him as Savior and claimed that they met him personally after his death from A.D. 33 to 1925.
3. More than 1,800,000,000 accepted him as Savior and claimed that they met him personally from 1925 until now and are alive today.

Now, let's total these: 3,800,000,643 human beings affirm that Jesus Christ is alive from the dead.

Put them in a courtroom, cross-examining 10 witnesses a day, would take 380,000,064 days to hear all their testimonies.

And every one of them would testify that Jesus is alive in their hearts.

TWENTY-SIX

Everything I Needed to Know
I Learned from My Dog

1. Never worry about what you are going to eat or where you are going to sleep; all will be provided for you.
2. Rest as often as you can. You must save your energy to chase the big cars of life.
3. Trust the One who feeds you; he always shows up at the right time.
4. Make time to take care of yourself; you're no good to anyone if there are stickers in your feet.
5. Love your Master and your pack.
6. Defend your Master and your pack.
7. Know all the dogs in your territory; some are your allies, and some are enemies. Wag your tail at both.
8. Satan owns the roadways.
9. Whatever looks interesting in the middle of the road may cost you a leg.
10. Never worry about what to wear.

11. Kiss those you love daily.
12. Howl when you feel like it.
13. Play hard.
14. Always be loyal.
15. Seek training from your Master every day.
16. Listen for your Master's voice even when you're sleeping; you never know when he has something for you to do.
17. Stick close to the house; it's where the love and the food come from.
18. If you're out wandering in the woods and you get lost, just sit and listen. Sooner or later you'll hear your Master whistle for you, and you'll know how to get back home.
19. Just because you can't see your Master doesn't mean he's not there.

—Martha Moody

TWENTY-SEVEN

Laughter-Silvered Wings

There hangs upon my wall in my home a beautiful plaque. It was given to me by James Irwin, the astronaut, who walked, leaped, and danced on the surface of the moon.

On the plaque is the great poem "High Flight," written by John Gillespie Magee Jr., a nineteen-year-old pilot who died in an air battle shortly after he wrote it.

I realize that the world is familiar with the poem, but I want to repeat it here for a reason.

Oh, I have slipped the surly bonds of earth,
And danced the skies on laughter-silvered wings;
Sunward I've climbed, and joined the tumbling mirth
Of sun-slit clouds—and done a hundred things
You have not dreamed of—wheeled, and soared, and swung
High in the sunlit silence. Hovering there,
I've chased the shouting wind along, and flung

My eager craft through footless halls of air.
Up, up, the long delirious, burning blue
I've topped the wind-swept heights with easy grace
Where never lark, nor even eagle flew.
And while, with silent, lifting mind I've trod
The high, untrespassed sanctity of space,
Put out my hand and touched the face of God!
　　　　　　　　　　—John Gillespie Magee Jr.

This magnificent triumph of a poem is a symbol of the soaring of the soul, when the Spirit becomes the winds beneath your wings, and you are not required to stoke continually the coals of dying embers of fading carnality.

I can truthfully attest that when I have dedicated my life to Christ, I have slipped the surly bonds of earth, and my soul has danced the skies on laughter-silvered wings.

I have climbed sunward and joined the tumbling mirth, wheeled and soared, and swung high in the sunlit silence.

I have heard the shouting wind and felt my spirit soar through footless halls of air.

I have sallied through the delirious burning blue and topped the windswept heights with easy grace, where never lark nor eagle flew.

And my silent, lifting mind has trod the untrespassed sanctity of space; and by Christ's saving grace, I have reached out and touched the face of God!

This is what happens when the Spirit of God free-flows through the corridors of the mind and soul of all who believe in him for salvation and satisfaction.

Before Jim Irwin died a too-soon death, I sat with him at the Breakers Hotel in Palm Beach, and we discussed his "High Flight" organization.

Jim went into an explanation of the organization's logo. It was two intersecting orbital paths around the earth. Each orbit was a highly elevated apogee (or high point), emphasizing the importance of elevated goals in God's enabling and man's outreach.

There was a vertical and a horizontal orbit. The vertical represents the mutual search between God and man. The horizontal orbit represents humankind's outreach to other humans.

At the point where the high points of each orbit meet, there is the cross. Yes! That is it, exactly! At the point of the highest aspirations of man hangs the Savior Jesus.

The base of the cross is rooted in the ground, symbolizing God's downward reach, clear into the earth, for broken humanity. The top of the cross points skyward, symbolizing the glorification of God by the Son's obedience and humankind's highest aspiration to glorify God in the highest. The outstretched arms of the cross represent God's loving arms reaching out to the last person at the last station at the farthest point away.

The job of the Holy Spirit, sometimes so lost in the dusty pages of our minute theology, is to energize all to whom these symbols allude.

Mankind, filled and refilled, empowered and outreaching, reenergizing our decadent symbols and ossified prewritten conclusions will stumble upon wonder after wonder. And every wonder will be true! It must destroy our wretched cleaving to carnal-based, myopic, concretized conclusions that God is finished with speaking to us and through us. That must die, and you are just the people to do it.

So long as we Christians of the twenty-first century do not slip the surly bonds of earth, we will never sunward climb. But, if we do, we shall be wheeling and soaring, and swinging and chasing the shouting wind along, and flinging through the footless halls of air . . . through the delirious burning blue, where never lark nor eagle flew, and trodding the high untrespassed sanctity of space, we reach out and touch the face of God.

Aye, if we do not do that, we shall continue wading in the mudbanks of mediocrity and clanging together in carnal division, and man-made mush of egoistic preacher-pride, while others less sophisticated and educated are used, as were the apostles of old, these artless and unsophisticated men . . . all used for the unbridled praise of his name!

I see the youth of the twenty-first century. They are set, ready to run, looking back at us, their hand reaching back for us to stretch and hand the baton we've been carrying.

In the name of the Christ of God, let us "lay aside every weight, and the sin which doth so easily beset us" and hand a well-carried baton to the reaching fingers of our children, and our children's children . . . so they may begin the great run down the chalk-line lane reaching out to the twenty-second and twenty-third and twenty-fourth centuries.

We have a world to win, and I confess my sin, and dare to begin again to win the souls of men. In the name of Christ! Amen! and Amen!

TWENTY-EIGHT

God, If You Have a Plan for My Life, Where Were You Last Thursday?

(Dr. Nelson Price gave me this title)
Romans 8:26–31

While vacationing in Glorieta, New Mexico, one summer, I heard a friend say, "If God has a plan for my life, where was he last Thursday?"

I'm not quite sure what miniature or super catastrophe had occurred in his life that previous Thursday, but somehow he was in a struggle between events as they are . . . and God as some people have presented him to be.

A young man came by to see me this last Thursday. It was a hot afternoon, so a large glass of iced tea was a welcome friend.

This young friend of our family broke from his usual pattern and slowed down into a quite uncharacteristic seriousness.

"This God business is driving me up the wall," he said.

"Is it a wailing wall?"

"No, I'm not that frustrated. It's only a wall to climb, so help me climb it."

"What is the toughest part of the climb?" I probed.

"How God could allow a child I know to be run over by a truck, driven by a drunk. I just can't seem to get it together, Dr. Jess. You're the preacher, you tell me."

The young man's troubled question is troubling lots of people. The idea behind the question of my Glorieta friend has been haunting me. "God if you have a plan for my life, where were you last Thursday?"

So I have with me the *Palm Beach Post* of last Thursday. It teems with man's hopes, frustrations, a few affirmations, and many questions.

A newspaper is the house in which live politicians, sports stars, city commissioners, oil companies, criminals, personal want ads, the nonhumorous "funny papers," justice, prevarication, some toasted tripe, taxation, and swampland. Men who appear in its pages too often seem to end up in serious turmoil, in court, or as the target of the guilt transferral of either the masses or some opposing political party.

God, where were you last Thursday?

Some readers of the *Post* might have read: "Polyurethane Home Burns: Two Die."

Why, God? Why should a father and a son die? Did you will it? Don't you control everything? Where were you when it happened?

Or they read: "Police: Man Set Afire While Alive."

Why, God? Did you will it? Don't you control everything?

Where were you when it happened? Where were you last Thursday?

Others read about how some local merchants rip off a lot of little widows, Social Security recipients, and some hard-pressed working people by putting less in containers than they advertise.

Why, God? Why should people be cheated and over-charged? Did you will it? Don't you control everything? Where were you when it happened?

I must give answer that God freely created free man, with no strings attached; then the nonpuppet man creates sin, and sin wrecks the life of free man, who becomes nonfree by the wrong use of the God-given freedom.

Sin is the culprit at the root of the act—not God.

God has a plan and a will. He does not will that any should perish—not a father or his son, but he does will that what happens as a result of man's act may result in God's glorification.

The formula never reads:

God's will = man's tragedy
    but
man's act = man's tragedy
    then
man's tragedy = God's will.

God's will isn't always the cause of man's tragedy, but it must always be the result.

If God is pulling the strings on my every move, I am not responsible. We have cried out against blaming Satan for our wicked propensity; now we protest the blaming of God for the sinfulness of man and society.

When you sin, Satan didn't do it, you did; when the results of your sin—or man's sin—cave in on you, God didn't cause it, you—man—caused it.

It wasn't God who killed six million Jews in Nazi Germany and eight million Christians in North Korea and China; ethnically inspired, God-rejecting men did it.

Reject God because of earthquakes and lightning?

I admit that it is difficult to explain the presence of wickedness in the world of a good God, but have you ever tried to explain the presence of goodness in a world of no God?

There is just no way to jam all the truth about this vastly complex world into one human brain. Many skulls have cracked wide open trying to house the answer to this one question. "Where were you last Thursday?"

The Hindu skull burst after calling it a conflict between reality and illusion.

The Zoroastrian brain exploded after defining it as a conflict between light and darkness.

The platonic mind was devastated after depicting it as a war between matter and spirit.

The Christian thought ran its course by defining it as a battle between God and Satan . . . but behind this obvious dualism stands God, the monism, the One Mind.

I cannot give you a neatly packaged little plan of tragedy, but I can assure you that out of the screams of birth comes a happy newborn child; out of the "My God, why . . ." of Calvary came the happy shout of "He is risen!"

Pain precedes pleasure. Hurt predates help. Law antidates love.

If you were allowed to be God for a day, having all knowledge and all power, what in this world would you change? Would you do away with the law of gravity that causes falls? Or warming fire that rages through our forests? Would you make our world whimsical, capricious, and lawless?

Would you do away with death and cause the writer to put down his pen, the artist his brush, and the surgeon his scalpel as we all slip into the lazy occupancy of an eternal, noncreative world?

What wonderful friends are fear and pain, if they cause us to move into an insecurity that will send us hurrying, hurrying to solve problems and heal hurts.

All good science is based on the fact that this world is insecure.

All good religion rests on the fact that we must prepare for the onrush of eternity.

It was God who took the cross (a tragedy) and made a dagger to knife death to death (a victory).

Look at Romans 8:28: "And we know that all things work together for good to them that love God." Actually, and very technically, the "all things" is not the subject of this sentence, but the object. F. F. Bruce says it really ought to read: "To them that love God, God works all things . . . for good."

The New English Bible ties the Holy Spirit into the subject of the verse from the previous verse, and it reads: "He pleads for God's own people in God's own way; and in everything, as we know, he cooperates for good with those who love God."

Barclay translates it, "God intermingles all things for good for those who love Him."

The older we get, the more personal history we can refer to that shows us the rhyme and reason for the "intermingling" of all things. Older people usually do not raise these questions—only the young with no personal history to which to refer.

And there is a knowledge that can see through this thing if you truly love God. "All things work together . . . to them that love God." The more the love, the more the understanding. The more I love the more I trust.

Epectitus wrote: "Deal with me as Thou wilt from now on. I am as one with Thee: I am Thine: I flinch from nothing so long as Thou dost think it is good. Lead me where Thou wilt. Wouldst Thou have me hold office or hate (translation mine) it, stay or flee, be rich or poor. For this I will defend Thee before men" (William Barclay, *The Letter to the Romans,* 118).

It was in that same spirit that Paul wrote "in all these things we are more than conquerors through him that loved us. For I am persuaded that neither death, nor life, nor angels, nor principalities, nor powers, nor things present, nor things to come, nor height, nor depth, nor any other creature, shall be able to separate us from the love of God, which is in Christ Jesus our Lord" (Rom. 8:37–39).

God's love is my clothing if I am naked.

God's love is my food if I am hungry.

God's love is my wealth if I am in poverty.

As Barth said, "Everything must work together, in order

that the man whom God loves may be fitted to participate in that good thing" (Karl Barth, *The Epistle to the Romans*, 320).

The love of God dares see everywhere on this side and on that side of every great riddle.

> Though the cause of Evil prosper, yet t'is
> Truth alone is strong
> Truth forever on the scaffold,
> Wrong forever on the throne—
> Yet, the scaffold sways the future,
> And behind the dim unknown,
> Standeth God within the shadow,
> Keeping watch above his own.
> —James Russell Lowell

TWENTY-NINE

Baptism Is a Holy Ordinance . . . However

My longtime and deeply loved friend, Charles Wellborn, sent a story that triggered my memories about experiences while baptizing. I know that it is a holy ordinance, not to be trivialized; but I must admit that some strange things can happen when someone enters a baptismal pool. An entire book could be written about the myriad human experiences in this once-in-a-lifetime spiritual exercise.

I can never forget the night Charles gave his life to Christ. He was a national debate champion, taught by the great Dr. Glen Capps of Baylor University. Charles was perhaps the most respected intellectual on our campus, but he was a professed atheist, or at least an agnostic.

We were having a prayer meeting in the Seventh and James Baptist Church. Several of us were burdened for a spiritual awakening to come to America and the world—and had been praying for many nights for this great awakening to come.

I remember my surprise, as if it were yesterday, when the campus scholar and agnostic, Charles Wellborn, joined us. I was sure that he had come to annihilate us with his intellectual wizardry and well-furnished vocabulary. When Charles spoke, the words flowed like warm oleaginous butter.

We entered into prayer, and it became quite fervent. Under my breath, I prayed for Charles. When it seemed that the prayer meeting was about to close, I heard this eloquent voice call out to God.

"O God, is there a place for a poor sinner such as I?"

Charles Wellborn's conversion story swept the Baylor campus. It was his conversion that convinced even skeptical Christians that God was up to something truly revolutionary at this stage in history.

Now we know the rest of the story.

A youth awakening started across America. I was at the founding of Youth for Christ in Winona Lake, Indiana, in 1945, which started the revival in the northern part of the United States.

I believe I was at the beginning of the awakening in the southern United States at the conversion of Charles Wellborn that same year.

Scores of young ministers preached in hundreds of churches throughout America. Elton Trueblood spoke of "The Authority of the Amateur," and he was most certainly typifying us with that appellation.

Charles became one of those preachers, as was I.

A big movement like this has its deeply moving experiences. It also has its humorous episodes. Some of them refer to baptism.

Charles wrote me about one of his less glorious days.

I went for a week of services in a church in Alabama. They had just completed a lovely new sanctuary. Departing from their usual Baptist practice, they had not built their baptistry behind the choir loft at the front of the church, but had constructed a baptismal pool, adorned with greenery, out into the sanctuary, at the left of the platform where the preacher and others sat.

The revival began well, with a number of converts on Sunday. Accordingly, the pastor decided to begin each evening of the revival . . . with a baptismal service. Everything went well until that Thursday evening. There was just one convert to be baptized—a sincere lady who, unfortunately, had a nervous nature.

Before the service on that evening, the pastor came to me, obviously a little agitated. "This lady," he said, "is terribly afraid of water. We may have problems, but I counseled her, and I think everything will be all right."

The service began. I was seated on the left of the platform just below the baptismal pool. The lights dimmed. The pastor came into the pool, backing up, leading with both hands the obviously terrified lady.

The congregation could not hear him, but from where I sat I could hear him, almost in desperation, saying, "It's all right. Just relax!"

The lady was quite ample. Indeed, she was about as wide as she was tall. The pastor was built just like her. He was ample also.

When they came to the center of the pool, he said to her, "Just relax. It's all right."

She did not relax. She was frozen solid—in the ice of fear. The desperate pastor, in whispers, admonished her, finally bursting out with, "Relax, dadgummit, relax!"

At that point she did relax, suddenly and precipitously. She fell back into the baptistry. The pastor followed her. And we had the spectacle of two small whales, floundering around in the water, trying to regain their feet! Sitting next to them, as the waves splashed, I was drenched from head to foot.

The congregation barely restrained their hilarity.

I preached while sopping wet!

The pastor did not attempt a baptism for the rest of the week, although there were quite a number of converts. I hope he eventually recovered his nerve.

Another episode in the parade of baptismal wonders took place in Pasadena, Texas. The pastor was D. B. Landrum, who now serves on the staff with Ed Young at Second Baptist Church of Houston, Texas.

On a quiet Sunday evening, the pastor was baptizing several people. Among them was a fashionable, dignified, attractive woman. She came into the baptistry, her beautiful face beaming, and her well-coiffed and quite lovely blonde hair shone stunningly.

Dr. Landrum looked at her beautiful hair closely, then said to himself, "That looks store-bought."

Shaking the quite earthly thought from his mind, he

proceeded to lower this lovely down into the water—only to see store-bought hair floating away across the baptistry!

Landrum's brilliant mind raced: "I can't lower a beautiful lady under the water and raise up a someone with grey hair. It is a bad testimony for baptism!"

So, with the lady still under the water, he took her with him—submarine style—in hot pursuit of the escaping wig! Finally, he caught up with the wig, put his right hand under the submerged beauty, caught the wig in his left hand, and rammed it onto her head.

Then, with a triumphant flourish, Landrum raised the glorious lady out of the water! The only problem was that he had put it on her sideways, thus leaving the impression that he had wrung her neck!

Who said being in the ministry wasn't fun?

THIRTY

Christ's Humble Entry

Sometimes He comes through a baby's cry;
Sometimes through the ache of pain;
Sometimes just before you die;
Sometimes through the gentle rain.

Sometimes He comes through a strong word;
Sometimes through a sudden gain;
Sometimes through the song of a bird;
Sometimes through the gentle rain.

Sometimes He comes through a thunder's blast;
Sometimes through the ear of summer grain;
Sometimes through the guilt of a sin long past;
Sometimes through the gentle rain.

I've heard His whisper softly on my ear;
I've had the gain, and the sudden pain;
I've felt Him wash away my deepest fear;
As I walked with Him in the gentle rain.

(Dedicated to the congregation of the Shepherd of the Hills Church, Porter Ranch, California.)

THIRTY-ONE

Captain Randy Willis

I have had more fun being the pastor of three great churches. All three had great people in them. I enjoyed all three.

Every pastor worth his salt deserves to be the minister of one, good, loving church. I served three like that.

A small story is applicable here. A man married two women, each of whom died. The cemetery plot placed them on each side of where he was to be buried. He was dying, and they asked him which of the two he favored.

"It is hard to say. I guess you'd better tilt me a little toward Tillie."

If I were asked as to which of the three I served, I would probably say, "Tilt me a little toward First Baptist, West Palm Beach."

There are reasons for that. They were a loving, tolerant-of-me, cooperative, supportive, friendly, can-do congregation. So much was accomplished there. The list is endless. The two-thousand-seat Chapel by the Lake outdoor amphitheater, a new sanctuary, the day school, Palm Beach Atlantic College, winning over a thousand teenagers and arranging to conduct services for 65,000 kids at the Palm Beach Raceway Rock Festival (baptized 168 in one rainy night in the Chapel by the Lake), a large educational building, mission churches, airplane ambulance for Brazil, money for a church in Saudi Arabia (never built—blocked by the Saudi government), emergency operating unit for Africa, furnishing the Bill Wallace Hospital operating room in Korea, building a floating church on the Amazon in Brazil.

An endless line of victories! All to the glory of Christ the Lord!

The services were sensational.

I shall always remember their faces.

One unforgettable one was a yacht captain. He came to the services in a Bristol—bright uniform, all bedecked with medals and jazzy epaulets. He looked like a South American dictator.

When I first met him, I introduced myself, and he stiffened in strict naval stiffness and announced that he was "*Captain* Randy Willis."

I told him that I got the rank but not the name.

He clarified the name as Randy Willis.

He never missed a service and always walked around the sanctuary so everyone could see him. He always sat near the front . . . a sight to behold . . . fully bedecked—and full of himself.

Every time he met someone, his announcement of his title could be heard all over the sanctuary.

One evening I was preaching about how Christ made himself of no reputation and humbled himself and took on the form of a servant. When I extended the invitation, several came forward, and we were rejoicing with them, and the service was about to end.

Suddenly, I noticed out of my quartervision someone moving to the aisle. It was the well-bedecked captain. His clear blue eyes riveted on me. Glorious tears rolling down his checks, he came straight to me, stopped, and slowly saluted. Then, just about a whisper, he croaked out the words: "Lowly seaman, Randy Willis, reportin' for duty, sir!"

He faithfully reported for duty till the day of his death . . . when he met the King of kings—who I believe, saluted the lowly seaman, Randy Willis.

THIRTY-TWO

One Hungry Child

Each day eighteen thousand children under five years of age die of starvation. You can feed one a day at no cost to you. Before you ask the table blessing, punch up thehungersite.com. A world map will appear. Then punch DONATE FREE FOOD.

A child will be fed two and one-half cups of healthy food. It is already paid for! After that, pray this little prayer at the table:

Some can eat, but have no meat.
Some have meat and cannot eat.
We have meat and can eat;
Thank you, Lord. Amen.

—Jess and Doris Moody

THIRTY-THREE

Miracles

Nothing is more wonderful than what happens when a head and an important book get together. Why question that Jesus could change water into wine?

I've seen the miracle of a person's brain putting facts into an inkwell and writing them on parchment, and a thousand years later the words leap from the page into a young person's brain, who transfers it from his/her brain into words and then transfers the words to a metal microphone through an instrument called a TV station, and the words are changed into electronic signals, then back into sounds and pictures which are hurled at the speed of light across a continent and channeled to a marvelous camera called the eye, and another receiving set called the ear—both of which are transmitted to the brain, where the words are decoded and translated into images and symbols which the receiving set can comprehend.

Actually, I think changing water into wine was quite a small miracle compared to what I have just described.

THIRTY-FOUR

The Super Bowl Choke
(Dedicated to my friend, George Allen,
"Coach"—the best!)
(A talk to Washington Redskins, Buffalo Bills,
Houston Oilers professional football teams)

"I'm choking on the smog. I'm choking on crowds of people jostling me, stepping on me, irritating me, cheating me, lying to me. Enough! It's choking me to death. I want out!"

That was his suicide note.

He hanged himself . . . and choked to death!

The Amplified Bible vivisects the choke: "I have told you these things so that in Me you may have perfect peace and confidence. In the world you have tribulations and trials and distress and frustration; but be of good cheer. Take courage, be confident, certain, and undaunted—for I have overcome the world. I have deprived it of the power to harm, have conquered it for you" (John 16:33).

Is that hot—or what?

The big goblin in life is pressure.

Pressure is defined by Webster as "the burden of physical, or mental distress."

Chokes occur more often in sports than anywhere else. Athletic games don't deal in the abstract, the perhaps, the maybes of life. Sports is measured by exactness, by yards, feet, inches, meters, goals, sidelines, with exact penalties for specific sins.

Pressure is that which turns a yearlong .328 hitter into a World Series goat who bats .110. It is that which makes a guy shoot four 64s in the Desert Classic and fail to make the cut in the Open. It sends a .900 shooter to the free-throw line with two seconds to play, and he can't draw iron in a three-to-make-two situation.

It makes an All Pro fumble on the goal line, and turns a number 1 seed at Wimbledon into a double-faulter.

It is known among athletes as "the choke," "the apple," "the grape," and "the goiter." The best line Howard Cosell, the old sportscaster, could come up with was, "He needs a throat specialist."

Our church sponsored the Laywitnesses for Christ group during the Olympics. Twenty-two medal winners stood on the platform of our church and told what Christ had done for them. Again and again, I heard Carl Lewis, Jackie Joyner, and many others tell of Christ's ability to keep them cool in the furnace, thus releasing all their abilities to operate at full capacity.

I had the joy of attending many of the Olympic events during that astounding week. In event after event, the performances of Olympians are seconds, minutes, inches, feet, yards, pounds, and points well below their personal best. I saw some world record holders finish fifth.

Jim Murray, my favorite sportswriter of the *Los Angeles Times* observed this. "Allen Fauerbach, a shot-putter, the record holder, was one of the American contingent. (The shot put team) were respectively, eight and one-half inches, one foot and eight inches, and more than two feet below their world best. In the world of shot putting, there are vast drop offs. Any one of the three (participants) could have won if he had come within a foot of his previous best."

Now, move over to the Super Bowl. I become amused when I hear predictions about who the winner will be. The chief maxim is what our old coach, Howard Wade, used to say, "Yea verily! He who choketh, loseth."

The classic example is how, a few years ago, Joe Namath outpsyched the fabled win machine, the Baltimore Colts. The Jets didn't have a chance, but they won. Outpsyched.

Muhammed Ali psyched his opponents into Silly Putty, fight after fight.

I am sure that even Jesus felt the temptation to choke as he waited for Calvary. Think of it. The sins of all the ages would be laid upon him the next day. All hell gave permission to every vile, evil demon to concentrate on him that night. They danced around him for hours, taunting him, trying to psyche him out.

Heaven waited breathlessly for the result. Bathing himself in prayer to the Father, he still felt the fearful welter of temptation-to-the-nth-power. Heaven's cheering section grew quiet. Eternity's ears could hear his heavy breathing all the way to the North Star. After an eternal minute, freighted with all of life hidden in it, he spoke: "Father," the voice echoed through eternity's vaulted hills and valleys, "if it can be possible, take this cup from me . . . *nevertheless* . . . (You can almost hear history squeaking as it turns on its hinges!

Never . . . the . . . less.) not my will . . . but . . .thine be done!"

Heaven roared its victory shout: "He didn't choke!"

Jesus would have made the world's greatest quarterback. With eighty thousand people cheering in the stands, he could have called and executed the perfect nonchoke play.

Jesus would have made the world's greatest pinch hitter in World Series history. Bases loaded, last of the ninth, he would have walked to the plate as cool as a springtime swimming hole.

The author of the Book of Hebrews drew the picture classically:

> Since we have such a huge crowd of men of faith watching us from the grandstands, let us strip off anything that slows us down or holds us back, and especially those sins that wrap themselves around our feet and trip us up; and let us run [free-footed] with patience the particular race God has set before us.
>
> Keep your eyes on Jesus, our leader and instructor. He was willing to die a shameful death on the cross because of the joy he knew would be his afterwards; and now he sits in the place of honor by the throne of God.
>
> —Hebrews 12:1–2 TLB

Then the author of Hebrews tells *us* not to choke:

> If you want to keep from becoming fainthearted and weary, think about his patience as sinful men did such terrible things to him. After all, you have never yet

struggled against sin and temptation until you sweat great drops of blood.

—Hebrews 12:3–4 TLB

Who was that guy who says the Bible isn't a relevant book? Hebrews tells you how to avoid the Super Bowl choke:

1. Keep your eyes on Jesus (Heb. 12:2).

When the howling crowd is jeering and booing, don't think of yourself. Think of Jesus—and how he reacted to all the pressure that hell could put upon him!

Another bit of advice on nonchoking, when life's big moment comes:

2. Think about patience. Look again at Hebrews 12:2.

When James and John were screaming into his ears the motto of those Sons of Thunder: "Rain fire on them!" Jesus cooled it by simply ignoring their attitude.

When the Royal Order of Rock Throwers and Guilt Transferers were ready to stone him for his straight preaching to the home folks, he calmly walked away.

When their cousins, down in Jerusalem, tried to kill a young girl for committing adultery, Jesus laid a little guilt trip of his own on them . . . then knelt down beside her, so the rocks aimed at her could hit him too.

There, they choked. Not Jesus.

When Herod could have sent an army to spear Jesus to death, Jesus called him "That fox," . . . and they choked.

When the trained debaters went after Jesus with their trick

questions about divorce, following Caesar, and dozens of other little legal ploys, they choked. He didn't.

Now look at another key to avoiding the Big Choke.

3. Take a new grip.

You say, "Where did you get that, from Dale Carnegie?"

No. From the Bible, the Book of Hebrews:

"So, take a new grip with your tired hands" (12:12 TLB).

Regrip the situation. Ask Christ to cure your withered hands . . . and he will.

Then, there's another word.

4. Stand firm on your shaky legs.

When Jesus told the crippled man to rise up and walk, he did it, and he didn't choke.

5. Mark out a straight course for your feet and the feet of others.

> Mark out a straight, smooth path for your feet, so that those who follow you, though weak and lame, will not fall and hurt themselves, but become strong.
>
> —Hebrews 12:13 TLB

When your shaky legs grow stronger, I know that you will be ready for your nonchoking.

Joshua walk!

See Joshua 1:3: "Every place that the sole of your foot shall tread upon, that have I (already) given unto you."

It's all yours, so don't choke!

THIRTY-FIVE

The Situation Is Hopeless— but Not Serious

I was having lunch alone for a change, and a young man came to my table and asked if I minded chatting with him. I told him to please join me but I had to leave shortly.

After he discovered that I was nonjudgmental in my attitude toward him, he began to speak freely—and deeply: "I really have given up on there being a good, benevolent God in this universe. I am about to go the Madalyn Murray O'Hair route."

"Proceed," I said, beginning to savor the first bite of my no-no dessert.

"I feed all the facts into the computer of my brain, and my mind finds the concept of a good God to be intellectually indigestible, especially that a carpenter from Nazareth could have anything to do with space capsules, moon rocks, and microbes. It is a mind-boggling mystery, and I've struggled with it so long that I've given up any hope of making sense out of it."

His question made me think of a statement from somewhere in my past: "Man's knowledge is something like an old hen's knowledge of a hundred-acre farm, as her whole life has been spent scratching in just one corner of it."

Some people have been filled with despair that they cannot force an ounce of meaning out of every one hundred pounds of pressure because of bombings, baby deaths, cancer killing young people, and the rape of an old woman.

So they decide to give up on believing in God and Christ and settle for a nontheistic good attitude toward the universe, the world, and the old hometown.

No more will faith in Christ and God be in their minds. They will accept the clear reality of the Golden Rule, and that will be quite enough to function in life.

I would be less than honest if I didn't admit that the complexity of life baffles me, literally stuns me out of my composure. A cosmos in which it would take 250,000 years to count the atoms in a pinhead is not exactly oversimplified. If there is that much to know about a pinhead, how much is there to know about a universe?

So the route of atheism or agnosticism is a statement that God and meaning are subjects too difficult to master, so they escape into the cave of ignorance or nonlearning concerning the subject.

Man has been staggered by the startling discoveries which began opening up to us in 1945, and it has reduced man's self-confidence and identity until he has become "a forked radish with a head fantastically carved"—that and nothing more.

Life to many has become a mystery, wrapped in a question, and sealed by an enigma. We can't seem to unscrew the unscrutable.

"So," I told the young man, "since things can't be figured out, you have given up on God—not believing there is mind before the universe, with the river of purpose running through it. You are giving up the idea that there is a worthwhile purpose to things that happen to us. You have decided that man is an accident of dust and not a child of God's eternal Spirit."

He had decided to be simply good without reference to God—good for no reason and toward no purpose. But how did that goodness get here?

Think of the goodness of Jesus. Where did all that loving, saving, caring, redeeming goodness come from? Could someone be that good, that wise, that healing—and be mistaken about where the goodness came from?

This sort of question and its obvious answer have caused millions of people to accept the way of Christ and the Christ of the Way. Christ's goodness is the heart of what makes Christ, Christ; love, love; and life, life.

I want to testify to you that I have seen with my own eyes tens of thousands of people who live the Christian life of Christ's goodness. I have seen it in the eyes of some dear people who have poured out into this pagan world as Jesuslike integrity and humanness which make the Christian life believable.

I have seen it in homes where what Christ taught as the Law of love is their daily fare. It was not Christianity defended; it was Christianity in action in living Incarnation. It was not a statement of faith; it was Christ in loving action.

I read where Jesus changed water into wine; I personally have seen him change creed into deed. If to defend the faith were mainly to argue for its credibility, few of us could help; but if to defend it is to exhibit its possibility, then every one of us can be involved.

This is taking Christ out of theological books and putting him in the city street. It is making it all come true now, *today,* instead of "once upon a time."

So, to the young man considering agnosticism, we commonly urge that his faith is like milk; either drink it down, or it will go sour very soon. You see, agnosticism is nothing but soured faith.

I remember the day I buried a twenty-five-year old girl, a product of our church. The funeral home was jammed with people giving the gift of their faith to those shattered members of the family. She had two tall, strong young brothers; her young fiancé was there, and dozens of young people were present.

I was glad to be able to say to them, "The situation is hopeless but not serious."

The agnostic mind can only say the first half of that sentence: "The situation is hopeless."

There she lay in that beautiful coffin, as pretty as any girl could ever be . . . but dead. "The situation is hopeless."

We stood on the green grass at the cemetery. Six handsome young men bore her body from the hearse to the gaping, awesome hole in the ground. "The situation is hopeless."

The barrenness on her mother's face; the ashened countenance of her father as he sat at graveside, looking longingly at the casket. "The situation is hopeless."

The heaving, shaking body of a brokenhearted brother. "The situation is hopeless."

Of course, the only thing to do is deny God, run to the retreat of doubt, flee to the hills of agnosticism because "the situation is hopeless."

But wait, at that funeral a prayer was prayed. "The situation is hopeless . . . but . . ." Wait!

The pastor said, "She has laid down a life she could not keep to take up a life she can never lose. We commit to earth only that which is mortal of Ellen Marie."

"The situation is hopeless—but . . ." Wait! Scriptures were read: "Let not your heart be troubled; ye believe in God, believe also in me. In my Father's house are many mansions" (John 14:1–2).

"The situation is hopeless . . . but not serious!"

"I saw a new heaven and a new earth. I John saw the holy city . . . I heard a great voice out of heaven saying, . . . God is with men" (Rev. 21:1–3).

THIRTY-SIX

Willing to Will
(A rap)

When I'm willing to will the great will of God,
I will want to want what you want me to want.
    Great will of God!
    Great thrill of God!
Willing and wanting your will, dear God!
Willing and wanting your will, dear God!

When I want to want what you want me to want,
I will want to do what you want me to do.
    Great will of God!
    Great thrill of God!
Wanting and doing your will, dear God!
Wanting and doing your will, dear God!

When I want to do what you want me to do,
I will want to go where you want me to go.

Great will of God!
Great thrill of God!
Going where you want me to go, dear God!
Going where you want me to go, dear God!

THIRTY-SEVEN

My Most Intriguing Person

On an ABC talk show, *Religion on the Line,* the host, Carol Hemingway, asked me, "Of all the people you have ever met or read about, who was the most intriguing?"

My reply was that everyone on earth is intriguing, if you look deeply enough. "I wrestle with your quick question for a deep answer. Harry Truman intrigued me because of his lack of self-obsession. Will Rogers, a distant cousin, intrigued me because of his guilelessness."

Then, it hit me. I knew the answer I would give.

George Washington Carver. Most moderns don't have a clue as to who he was.

He was a small, humble American who revolutionized the economy of the South. Born one year before slavery was outlawed, 1864, this quiet little man was orphaned in infancy because his mother was kidnapped, and raised by his Uncle Moses and Aunt Sue Carver. They loved him, gave him a sense of worth, and taught him to have confidence in his mental powers under God.

As a boy, he walked alone in the woods and loved the out-of-doors world. Up from abject poverty, he was educated and graduated from Iowa State College of Agriculture and Mechanical Arts.

He became an accomplished artist. One of his paintings, "The Yucca," won major recognition at the Chicago World's Fair of 1893. But art was not to be his major contribution.

A newly formed college in Alabama, Tuskegee Institute, invited him to teach. Booker T. Washington was its first president. At Tuskegee, Carver invented or discovered several major contributions to the world: *Penol* and a cure for infantile paralysis. George Washington Carver discovered over 300 uses for the peanut, 118 uses of the sweet potato, and many from the soybean. These included cosmetics, face powder, lotion, shaving cream, vinegar, cold cream, printer's ink, salad oil, instant coffee, synthetic tapioca and egg yoke, flour, paints, nontoxic colors from which crayons were developed.

Once Carver was visited by Henry Ford, who offered him a large salary to come to Dearborn and do his research. Carver refused because he wanted to stay and help his people.

Calvin Coolidge, Franklin Roosevelt, and many others came to this place of wonderment, where a humble black man converted the lowly peanut into a booming economy.

Once Carver was introduced by Dr. Willis D. Weatherford, who was quite generous with his introduction.

Carver's response: "I always look forward to introductions to learn something about myself."

The little man, in a high-pitched voice, went on:

Years ago, I went to my laboratory and said, "Dear Mister Creator, please tell me what the universe was made for?"

The Great Creator answered, "You want to know too much for that little mind of yours. Ask something more your size, little man."

Then I asked, "Please, Mr. Creator, tell me what man was made for?"

Again the Great Creator replied, "You are still asking too much. Cut down on the extent and improve on the intent."

So then I asked, "Please Mr. Creator, will you tell me what the peanut was made for?"

"That's better, but even then, it is infinite. What do you want to know about the peanut?"

"Mr. Creator, can I make milk out of a peanut?"

"What kind of milk do you want? Good Jersey milk, or just plain boardinghouse milk?"

"Good Jersey milk."

And then the Great Creator taught me to take the peanut apart and put it together again. And out of that process have come forth all these products!

Three and a half ounces of peanuts produce one pint of rich milk or one quart of boardinghouse "blue john" milk.

In 1921, George Washington Carver spoke before the United States Senate Ways and Means Committee in the nation's capitol. He spoke one hour and forty-five minutes.

When he finished, the chairman asked Carver where he learned all these things.

Carver answered, "From an old book."

"What book?" asked the senator.

"The Bible," Carver answered.

The senator asked, "Does the Bible tell about peanuts?"

"No, sir," Dr. Carver answered, "But it does tell about the God who made the peanut. I asked him to show me what to do with the peanut, and he did."

In 1924, Dr. Carver spoke at the Marble Collegiate Church. The hearers never forgot that day. He said:

"God is going to reveal to us things he never revealed before if we put our hands in his. No books ever go into my laboratory. The things I am to do and the way of doing it are revealed to me. I never have to grope for methods. The method is revealed to me the moment I am inspired to create something new. Without God to draw aside the curtain, I would be helpless. Only alone can I draw close enough to God to discover his secrets."

Once Carver was asked to share some of his observations about God. Carver responded:

As a very small boy, exploring the almost virgin woods of the old Carver place, I had the impression someone had just been there ahead of me. Things were so orderly, so clean, so harmoniously beautiful. A few years later in the same woods, I was to understand the meaning of this boyish impression.

Because I was practically overwhelmed with the sense of some Great Presence. Not only had Someone *been* there, but Someone *was* there.

Years later, when I read in the Scriptures, "In him we live and move, and have our being," I knew what the writer meant. Never since have I been without this consciouness of the Creator speaking to me . . . the out-of-doors has been to me more and more a great cathedral in which God can be continuously spoken to and heard from.

Man, who needed a purpose, a mission, to keep him alive, had one. He could be . . . God's coworker.

My attitude toward life was also my attitude toward science. Jesus said one must be born again, must become as a little child. He must let no laziness, no fear, no stubbornness keep him from his duty.

If he were born again, he would see life from such a plane he could have the energy not to be impeded in his duty by these various sidetrackers and inhibitions. My work, my life, must be the spirit of a little child seeking only to know the truth and follow it.

My purpose alone must be God's purpose—to increase the welfare and happiness of his people. Nature will not permit a vacuum. It will be filled with something.

Human need is really a great spiritual vacuum, which God seeks to fill.

With one hand in the hand of a fellowman in need, and the other in the hand of Christ. He could get across the vacuum, and I became an agent. Then the passage, "I can do all things through Christ who strengthens me," came to have a real meaning.

As I worked on projects which fulfilled a real human need, forces were working through me which amazed me. I would often go to sleep with an apparently insoluble problem. When I woke, the answer was there.

Why then should we who believe in Christ be so surprised at what God can do with a willing man in a laboratory? Some things must be baffling to the critic who has never been born again.

By nature, I am a conserver. I have found nature to be a conserver. Nothing is wasted or permanently lost in nature. Things change form, but they do not cease to exist.

After I leave this world, I do not believe I am through. God would be a bigger fool than even a man if he did not conserve what seems to be the most important thing that he has yet done in this universe. This kind of reasoning may aid the young.

When you get your grip on the last rung of the ladder, and look over the wall as I am now doing, you don't need your proofs.

You see. You know you will not die.

In 1939, George Washington Carver was awarded the Roosevelt Medal, with the declaration: *"To a scientist humbly seeking the guidance of God, and a liberator to men of the white race as well as the black."*

George Washington Carver remarked: *"The secret of my success? It is simple. It is found in the Bible. 'In all thy ways acknowledge Him, and He shall direct thy paths.'"*

Perhaps now you know why he was my most intriguing person.

THIRTY-EIGHT

Dinner With J. C. Penney

I am now an older minister, and I have given 50-plus years to the preaching of the Word and watching human beings do their thing during their brief time on stage. My life was turned around by several people I was privileged to meet.

Once, I was offered the presidency of a major company, which would have required that I leave the ministry.

The Spirit forbade it.

I stayed in the ministry.

On another occasion, I was asked to run for Congress.

The Spirit forbade it.

I stayed in the ministry.

Shortly after the second event, I had lunch with J. C. Penney.

I recounted those two experiences and asked him if I had done the right thing.

He looked at me for a long time in silence. In fact, the

silence became almost embarrassing. I became concerned about him and asked if he were all right.

"Yes, I am quite fine. I must tell you that I was faced with that decision a long time ago. I was just sitting here, in all this affluence of the Everglades Club (where we were dining), and thinking back a long time before—and wondering if I had made the right decision when I was quite young. That same decision confronted me. I chose business, but business as a ministry. Since then, I have given 70 to 90 percent of my income to the cause of Christ and man . . ."

He then shifted in his seat, and faced me full on.

"Young man, do you tithe?"

I was happy to tell him that since we turned down the presidency of the company, Doris and I had doubled-tithed to the cause of Christ and man.

Then he said something I have never revealed before this writing—and I write it as humbly as I know how.

J. C. Penney looked squarely at me and said, "Young man, before God, I wish I were you!"

I was too embarrassed to respond. I did not know what to say. I excused myself, and stepped outside the club, leaned against a building and wept out my gratitude to God.

It was a "Thou Moment" in my life.

Have you had a "Thou Moment" in your life?

You can.

How?

By giving largely to the futures of tens of thousands of boys and girls and men and women who will parade through eternal history and will follow in that glorious train of thousands of youngsters who have found their way to answer Christ's call to be pastors, missionaries, and godly businesspeople . . .

The Spirit is confronting you now: "WORLD CHANGERS, ONE AND ALL!"

THIRTY-NINE

Where Do You Hang Your Hang-ups?

(A sermon outline I stole from my son Patrick, a better preacher than I ever was. After all, he owes me! Oh, the joys of paternal plagiarism! All work and no plagiarism makes Jess a dull preacher. The filler is mine, not to be plagiarized by anyone. As everyone knows, plagiarism is a despicable, disgusting thing to do, unless it is from your son, who owes you! Now, the public words I said beginning with the above.)

There is only one thing more disgusting to decent society than for a son to steal from a father, a sport of choice engaged in by millions of legitimatized-by-birth sons and daughters.

I sense a small jolly in my gizzard as I reciprocate just this once (and any other time I choose) to steal from my son.

My son Patrick is a former actor and director in the motion picture business. He outmarried himself by taking as his bride Amy Jingst, one of the most kind, loving young women you could ever meet.

God, in his wisdom, must have thought, *This boy is going to need some help, considering his genes and paternity, so I will create a special helpmate for him.*

God, in his infinite wisdom, has given them three children: Christopher, Sean, and Jessica.

A few years ago God called Patrick into the ministry ("From make-believe to the real stuff!"). He started over, got an education, and became the executive pastor at the Shepherd of the Hills Church in Porter Ranch, California. I happened to be the pastor.

If you believe this is an easy, smooth-running relationship, you are terribly mistaken. We are very different, but we love and respect each other about 70 percent of the time. Patrick preaches when I am away.

Each summer, Doris and I go to our little summer Valhalla in Glorieta, New Mexico. Seventy-five hundred feet up (with ground underneath, of course). It is a place of pure air, playful animals—like Moe, Larry, and Curly, our squirrels, who chase one another in circles without becoming dizzy. Or Manny, Mo, and Jack, our rabbits who dash out to be seen for a fleeting instant, take bows, and blow back into the woods. And Fred and Alice, our two old crows who live on a high branch at mountaintop, clearly visible from my front porch.

Then there was Ralph, my lovely old friend, a bear, who visited our garbage can each morning just before dawn. I am an early riser, so I would talk with him—and, so help me, it's true; so long as I would talk with him, he would stand on his hind legs and listen—paying more attention to me than some of our church members do. When I finished talking, he would drop back on all fours and walk to the next garbage can.

This year, when we came back to Glorieta, Bill Hendricks, my neighbor, told me that some hunter saw Ralph in the woods and brought him down. I cried. I had lost the best listener to my stories and comments.

It was sad. I still look for him in the predawn light. I'll swear I've seen his form moving gently among the forest groves.

"That's nice, you say, and touching; but when are you going to get to that sermon you stole from your son?"

Look, I'm getting old.

I've earned the right to ramble.

OK, let's start over.

Where to Hang Your Hang-ups
(A sermon outline plagiarized from my son.)

On Friday evenings at 11 P.M. in Glorieta, Doris and I clear our schedule. Patrick is preaching from our church on national television.

The president couldn't schedule an appointment with us at that time. It is TV time in the mountains.

Now Patrick *is* good, but I never expected a message, an outline, to be so upbeat, so cogent, so unique, so relevant, as this one.

So, when better sermons are preached, I'll steal them—and with senile alacrity!

Patrick's text was Galatians 2:20: "I am crucified with Christ: nevertheless I live; yet not I, but Christ liveth in me; and the life which I now live in the flesh I live by the faith of the Son of God, who loved me, and gave himself for me."

Patrick's first point: Hang your Hang-ups Where He Hung Up!

When the reality of that point crashed into my psyche, something spoke, sang, shouted, and echoed in my soul that the Lord literally, physically, psychologically, emotionally, and spiritually felt the crush, the weight, the fearful welter and swelter of my personal sin. He actually took the pain of a wickedness that touched and burned his holy soul with feel of fire against his righteous flesh. And it was a fire I *caused* and his tender being adopted, took unto his bosom, Jess Moody's evil crimes against God.

My thoughts, plottings, greeds, lusts, and rebellions; and Jesus experienced the pain of the blaze of my sin that seared to the inner core of his absolute and unquestioned holiness. That pristinely pure, sweet, kind, holy Son of God felt the reverberation of evil echoing its horrid breath through the chambers of the holy temple of his body!

And I, Jess Moody, pastor of a church, dealing with human problems every day, preaching from my pulpit that the chains of sin had been broken—and, all the while, I could hear the rattling of my own chains! I realized that my *ego* had to be hung up where he hung up.

Look again at Patrick's text. Only this time, put the word *ego* everywhere Paul uses a personal pronoun. This beats Freud by a light-year.

EGO (Edging God Out): "EGO is crucified with Christ, nevertheless EGO lives; yet not EGO; but Christ lives in EGO; and the life EGO lives in the flesh, EGO lives by the faith of the Son of God, who loved EGO and gave himself for EGO."

Oh, look at this with clear eyes!

There can be no victory over drug addiction, sexual addiction, alcoholism, or gossip addiction until you openly confess that addiction, ask for forgiveness, and saddle it right on Christ's back, to be pack-carried-by-Jesus right out of your life!

Hang your hang-ups where he hung up!

The second point of Patrick's sermon, which I stole, is: If you hang your hang-ups where he hung up, then you must hang in there because he hung in there for you.

Human beings are the targets of their own inventions. Every new item on the market is not an unmixed blessing. They help and they weary the psyche.

An extreme example is virtual reality. VR is a computer-based experience that simulates real life. Users sometimes wear goggles that give the illusion of moving through a real place at a real time, with an ever-changing view.

With VR, one can duel or dance with a computerized figure . . . or play pitcher for the Los Angeles Dodgers, or be the quarterback for the Denver Broncos.

Think of it! A simulated experience! Now there's something for the Christian to think about!

I can put on my goggles, turn on my Virtual Reality machine, and *pretend* that I am feeding the hungry, *pretend* that I am in Indonesia as a missionary, *pretend* that I am deep in prayer, *pretend* that I am winning souls to Christ, or *pretend* that I am giving 90 percent of my income to God's work!

Come to think of it, millions of Christians engaged in Virtual Reality for hundreds of years before there was such a thing. My, how inventive and ahead of all science we are!

We can commit the sins of omission and think we didn't. Think what that will do to take away the feelings of guilt! Fantastic!

It won't take away our actual guilt, but it will be a glorious palliative to our consciences. We can give without giving, go without going, participate, and never cease couch—or pew—potato—ing!

Glory Hallewhoppee! Praise Jesus! I will have the feeling of being in the Amazon jungle . . . and never break a sweat!

This age of illusory everything—acting as if we really did it—can do wonders for calming down that sense of unease when the pastor preaches about sinnnn! (O shudder!)

We can keep our convictions in a concoction of continual chloroform and, at the same time, keep us open to the possibility of measuring our spirituality by how *close* we came to almost doing it.

A mature Christian can be one not only "virtually realitied" but *skirt* dangerously close to *actual realitizing.*

The new Pharisaism will state it thusly: "I don't think Jim is much of a Christian. He doesn't even come close to actualizing. I thank God that I nearly concretized last week. I'm growing in grace! Praise the Lord! I nearly did something for God!"

It is patently strange that the most relevant and applicable quote to this situation is something Father Divine said, a pretender-to-be-God of the last generation: "Too many of us metaphysicians don't know how to *tangibilitate!*"

Maybe these kinds of virtual reality Christians could form their own actors' guild. They could give awards, not Oscars or Emmys but Hypos, and the reviewers could be called "Hypocritics."

I can hear it now! "In the category of Best Actor in a Continuing Series, the award goes to Deacon Joe Jones of the First Church of the Last Chance, in Pigeon Prong, Arizona, for thirty-two years of almost tangibilitating and never being caught in one inconsistency—a truly amazing record of virtual realitizing."

Lock this in. There will be no "well dones" from Jesus to anyone but those who hang in there and truly incarnate the living Jesus in their heart of hearts! Lock this in!

Patrick then hit us with his third zinger: If you hang your hang-ups where he hung up . . . and hang in there, then you can hang out with God's people!

I define "hanging out with God's people" as Christians enjoying themselves when nobody is looking. Much of so-called Christian fellowship is too terribly unidirectional, in which the Christian who does all the talking has read one chapter more in the newest fad Christian book-of-the-month. Today, a prophet is one who is one book ahead of the rest of us.

There is a place for unidirectionalism—like Sunday worship. You know about Sunday worship—where the pastor is asked to be the research lab technician, who brings us a report of his findings, then admonishes us to go into tangibilitating "out there in the lost world!"

I'm struggling to say more than can be said by mere words here. There are concepts that break the backs of human words, and this is one of them: It is better illustrated than defined.

There is an electronic term that will, at least, point at it. It is *bandwidth*. *Bandwidth* is the capacity of a wire or radio frequency to carry information, often expressed as "bits per second."

For instance, a regular phone call requires a bandwidth of sixty-four thousand bits per second. The more bandwidth per second a system has, the better.

I probe my own heart on this "hanging out with God's people" to mean "What is my bandwidth of joy, love, hope, affirmation, and encouragement? How much does the bit-o-meter of my Christian life carry?"

Perhaps a revival is the conglomeration of Christians, with extra bandwidthing that transfers megabits of maxi-love, maxi-joy, maxi-encouragement, and maxi-hope that starts a maxi-fire that spreads to a maximum number of people in a conflagration of maxi-mega flame of the "love of God spread abroad by the Holy Spirit!"

Maybe that is revival!

You see, "Christian fellowship" is not a bunch of well-washed, overly insured Republicans "false kissing" (ummm-wahhh!) one another on the cheek. Maybe the way you can tell how long they have been members of the church is how deep their dimples are—those cheek cavities put in the face by millions of false ummm-wah kisses delivered during holy hugs in holy huddles.

Revival is not how many holy hugs—and free rubs—are delivered during some Bible conference but how many hurts are healed, heavinesses of spirit lifted, hopes stirred, hells escaped, and heaven's reservations made! That is revival.

As Patrick moved through his message, he delivered another grape from this luscious cluster: If you hang your hang-ups where he hung up and hang in there and hang out with God's people, then and only then can you hang loose!

The deep calm won't come until the deep hurts are healed, deep doubts are sealed, deep faith congealed, and deep peace revealed. Then and only then can you hang loose!

Like Paul. When they were about to behead him, if you had taken his pulse, you would have shaken your head and your watch in disbelief. It would have been a perfect seventy-two.

Like Stephen. They stoned him. He looked up to heaven and saw Jesus. After Jesus' resurrection the Bible says Jesus was seated, seated at the right hand of the Father . . . but wait! What's this?

When God's boy, Stephen, was stoned for standing up for Jesus, Steve, God's faithful little deacon, saw Jesus standing up for him!

When you know things like that happen, it isn't too tough to stand up for him who will stand up for you . . . and then you can *hang loose!*

FORTY

On Preaching

Preach as if the house is on fire, and you are the only one who knows the way out.

Preach as if you were the first witness of the open tomb.

Preach as if you were Paul, just before he was beheaded.

Preach as if you were a teenage girl who just heard from the one she loves, "I love you too."

Preach as if you were Lazarus, thirty seconds out of the tomb.

Preach as if you were Simon Peter, that fiery-eyed prophet from Pentecost's pulpit.

Preach as if the open tomb were yesterday, Pentecost this morning, and the Second Coming tomorrow.

Preach as if a deadly epidemic were in a children's ward and you just ran in with the serum.

Preach with the wonder of a child in Santa's lap.

Preach as if Jesus is sitting on the third row of your congregation.

Preach as if you were the town gossip in Bethany and you just heard about Lazarus coming back from the dead.

Preach as if you have just heard that Uncle Gotrocks has died and left it all to you.

Preach as if Jesus had just washed your feet.

Preach as if your son has come home from the war—safe!

Preach as if you were Martha fixing dinner for Jesus.

Preach as if you were Mary in the garden and just discovered that it was Jesus—not the gardener.

Preach to people who are at the end of their rope; don't give them the history of hemp.

Preach as if you were baptized five minutes ago.

Preach as if Jesus were on the telephone and said, "Get out there and tell them what I told you—and do it *now!*"

FORTY-ONE

Jim Ryan's Greatest Run

Note: This is a part-truth, part-fiction combination of several missionary aviators' stories—more truth than fiction.

Jack Mitchell had been a missionary to Brazil for several years. Brazil haunted him until he answered the call to share the gospel in a tough, unchartered area. He flew hundreds of flights to deliver medicine and bring sick people to the little hospital in Porto Velho. The faithful little Cessna was kept in as fine condition as Jack could make it.

If the engine quits over the jungle and you survive the crash, you could have a one-hundred-mile walk through the jungle. The anacondas or the jaguars would see that you didn't make it.

One missionary made it one mile from his crash site before a jaguar hand landed on his back, cracked his skull like a pecan, and ate the meat in the pecan, the brain. Missionary aviators don't think of things like that. They just fly, and fly, and fly—day after day. Some of those planes are thirty years old, and they fly daily. What days the missionary pilot isn't flying, he is repairing, almost with a pair of pliers and bailing wire, and sometimes that's about it.

One day, while working on a plane, Jack noticed a man trotting toward him from out of the jungle. He was obviously from the interior. He explained to Jack that someone had dropped a book from the giant bird that he flew. It was a Bible. Missionaries would sometimes do that while flying over a village in the deep interior.

This man had risked his life to come this far. Not only the jaguar, the anaconda, but there were also the cannibals, yes, cannibals in Brazil in the twentieth century.

There are hundreds of stories about the dark interior of the jungle. One of them was about the missionary who stumbled upon a large munitions cache that the Communists were storing up to supply a planned coup. Missionaries are not supposed to become involved in any interior politics. This one hurried to Brasilia, the capitol, and reported it only to the president, and the coup was averted. Those are stories missionaries don't tell because antimissionary reaction can come from the victor in battle, and the missionary dare not be identified with any political faction.

This man had come to Jack Mitchell, the Bible dropper, and asked him to come to the people and teach from the Jesus Book. Only one person in the tribe could read—and not too well, at that.

"Would you send more Jesus Books and send people to

teach them how to read and to tell them what the Jesus Book was all about?"

Jack kept the man there for a few days, gave him food, a few Jesus picture books, and a promise that he would come into the interior, one year from that day; but the only way that village could be opened up would be for them to clear a landing field for the plane to land. Then he could come, bring Jesus Books, teachers to teach them how to read, and bring doctors or nurses.

Jack had drawn pictures, with specifications of the size of the landing strip and how to do it. He also pledged that he would drop some tools to help them cut down the trees and clear the area. The man agreed.

Jack had named him Jim Ryan after the great American runner.

The day came that Jim Ryan was to make the run with the word about the agreement, the specifications, some medical supplies, and some food.

Jack thought of the Indian who ran from Nashville to New Orleans to warn Andrew Jackson about the planned British attack. He had but a few days to get there. As he started to run, they called out to him, "God bless your legs as you run!" The Indian made it, and Jackson thwarted the invasion.

As Jim Ryan left on the run of his life, Jack shouted to him, "God bless your legs as you run!"

About a month later, Jack packed up the creaky old Cessna with the tools, bounced out of the short runway, flew nearly an hour over the jungle, dropped the tools, a few medical supplies, a few Jesus Books, and some candy for the children. On his way back, Jack felt total exhilaration over the plans and the drop.

I hope Jim Ryan made it through, he thought. *God bless his legs as he runs.*

Mary, Jack's wife, wasn't too uneasy about Jack. He had flown many missions over the jungle, and sometimes he was a little overdue, but he tried not to be late getting in, lest she be overly concerned.

She did feel better when she heard the sound of his returning flight.

Ysedo worked with them at the missionary base. He came in, and said, "Miss Mary, you better come!" She went outside.

The plane was flying in giant circles around the village, then out over the jungle, then back over the compound. Mary couldn't fathom it. It took long lazy circles.

Jack usually flew right in because he wanted to save as much gas as he could, but these long, lazy circles?

Finally, the plane was circling near the strip, and the engine quit, and the Cessna glided into a field a mile or so away and flipped over on its back.

They rushed to the plane and found Jack dead. It was a heart attack.

A few weeks later Mary was packing her things to return to the states. She had given away most of his things to the other friends who had been so faithful to the mission station.

While going through Jack's briefcase, she found his diary, sat down and wept as she read the pages. Finally she came to his recounting the full agreement with Jim Ryan, the agreement that one year from the date of the writing, a plane would land on the landing strip and someone would stay there and teach about the Jesus Book and bring medical supplies.

Paul Henderson was a successful businessman in Texas. God had called him to preach, then to be a missionary. He was especially interested in missionary aviation. He was sent by the Southern Baptist Foreign Mission Board to take Jack's place.

He wasn't an experienced pilot at the time, but he was trying to learn as fast as he could because his mission was already spelled out.

There was much work to do. And so little time.

Paul practiced the delicate art of cross-control landing, a method of causing a plane to lose altitude fast without losing control. This was essential for landing in short runways in the jungles.

Paul and his wife, Sarah, did their feverish work to get established in Porto Velho. The people loved their easy openness, Sarah's cooking, and the parties to get the people familiarized with the new missionary family.

It worked. Usually, on a missionary field the natives are highly responsive. Not always, but here in Porto Velho, they were lovely, gentle, friendly people, anxious to please.

It was two days until the year Jack's agreement was to be fulfilled. The Cessna was loaded to the gunnels: Jesus Books, children's books, medical supplies.

"I don't know if Jim Ryan made it through, or if they have cleared the landing strip. I could have made a trial run, but there is just so much money for gasoline."

Paul was concerned but dogged in his determination. "If they have kept their word, and we don't show up, all credibility will be lost."

Paul was up at 5:00 A.M., checking everything twice. He ate a quick breakfast, not wanting to waken anyone.

The gray streaks of early dawning framed his serious face. His morning prayer was centered around the Gospel of Luke, chapter nine, where it was said of Jesus: "He steadfastly set his face toward Jerusalem."

Jesus kept his word. He showed up.

The main battle for bringing Christ's light to these people is just simply setting my face to go to Jim Ryan's village and showing up. Have they built the runway? Did they make it long enough?

Paul's mind rehearsed cross-controlling.

There wasn't room enough in that plane for a mouse to hiccup—just an incredible amount of stuff, with Paul squeezed in.

Sarah was soon up and running. Several of the natives had come. They all knew the story. They were there to see if the American missionary would keep Jack's word. This was terribly important to the image of the integrity of the mission.

When everything was ready, Paul kissed Sarah, hugged the people, then used all of his strength to get into the Cessna. *Flying is hard enough, without all this paraphernalia,* Paul thought.

Then, shaking that out of his mind, he looked out of the plane, yelled, "Clear!" then set the throttle slightly open, pulled out the carburetor heat, pushed the starter, and the loud burst of the engine cracked the quietude of the early dawn.

He bowed his head and said a prayer of commitment.

"Secular people will think I am nuts, Lord; but we know that Christ is the Living Way for all mankind. Maybe these people have cleared out the runway, maybe they haven't, but I ask that you help me keep Jack's word with them. This is the day Jack promised to be there. I am to go in his place."

The doubts began to flood his mind.

"What am I doing here? What is this all about? Is this Cessna overloaded? What will it do with this overload, when I cross-control?"

Every doubt. Then Paul thought of the morning prayer, "He steadfastly set his face to go to Jerusalem." He rammed in the throttle.

The Cessna roared out its defiance to the doubts Satan had put in Paul's mind. As the plane turned toward the runway, "We are on our way to Jim Ryan, Brazil, Lord!" The silver sird began to roll. Slowly at first. She was pretty heavily loaded. Then, gaining speed, Paul looked at the end of the runway. It looked closer than ever before. The silver lady picked up speed. Thirty. Forty. Fifty.

Paul eased the wheel back. She bounced once, twice, three times. On the third bounce, she wobbled skyward, clearing the trees at the end of the runway by a few feet.

Paul circled the plane back over the field. There was Sarah, good old Sarah, waving all the encouragement her heart could muster.

"God, you know how much I love that woman!"

The fog was doing what it always did that early in the morning, hugging the trees below. The compass moved slowly westward as the bird climbed in the morning air.

Paul adjusted the airfeed and aimed it right at his face, wakening every pore. The sun was orange to red, peeking over the horizon.

Paul checked his map, compass, used the ruler, drew a line from Porto Velho to Jim Ryan's village, then wrote on the line, "Jack's promise!"

The jungle below always looks like fingers reaching up to grab you and pull you down. A little time passed. Paul checked his location, heading, crosswind correction on the compass. The wind was usually pretty still this early in the morning; and if there were to be any, it picked up about nine or ten.

"Lord, please, this is pretty wild. Expecting Jim Ryan to get through, expecting the people to build the runway. If it's not there, we've gone to a lot of trouble for nothing."

"Stuff it, Paul!"

"Steadfastly set his face."

Five minutes. Nothing sighted yet.

Four minutes. Nothing.

Three minutes. Blank.

Two minutes. There is supposed to be a hump, not a hill, not a mountain—just a hump just this side of the runway—if it's there!

"Did those people have the fortitude to build that sucker?"

One minute out.

No runway.

Paul pulled back on the wheel, to get a little perspective with more altitude.

As the silver bird topped her climb, Paul saw it!

The best jungle runway he had ever seen!

God did bless old Jim Ryan's legs!

But . . . the runway was pretty short.

To come in as slowly as possibly, Jim opted for the old-fashioned rectangular approach—only slightly lower. Instead of fifteen hundred feet when she was parallel to the final approach, Jim came in at twelve hundred.

Here he cut the engine. She glided down the downwind leg, went into the first turn at about six hundred instead of eight, then just a hundred feet above the trees.

The runway was pretty short. Could old silver bird handle this weight during cross-control?

Paul pushed the left rudder and turned the wheel to the right, and the nose down. She shuddered as she took this awkward position to lose altitude fast. When she would begin to tremble, Paul would uncross. When she smoothed out, he would cross-control again.

Shudder-smooth . . . shudder-smooth. The trees were coming up fast. Paul had to clear them. Shudder-smooth, level her out.

He gave the engine a small burst. He thought he might clear those threatening branches dead ahead. A little throttle, gently back on the wheel. *Clear!* By five feet!

Gliding in and plop! on the ground!

Paul cut the engine, breathed a combination prayer and sigh. He then burst into tears. "This is for you, Jack!"

The natives were running as hard as they could. Paul didn't know it, but Jim Ryan was the first happy, crying face looking in on Paul!

And that is how the first church was planted at Jim Ryan Village.

FORTY-TWO

Out of Gas and Dropping Fast!

Romans 8:28

Jim Baker had graciously offered to fly us—*us* being O. D. Hall, Barry Schahn, Henry Brandt, and me—to Tampa to do a television program.

The flight was beautiful all the way, but when we arrived in Tampa, there were overcast skies with a four-hundred-foot ceiling. This low ceiling caused Jim to decide against landing at the Clearwater Executive Airport and to divert to Tampa International.

As we negotiated the approach through the thick fog bank, Jim suddenly determined that he was slightly off course for an easy landing and decided that he would go around again for another approach.

When we ascended out of the fog bank into the bright sunshine and began circling to prepare for a second approach, suddenly Jim's voice rang out, "Thank You, Lord!"

He showed us a small mirror that reflected the status of the landing gear. The nose wheel was locked in a half-forward position and would not extend. This made any idea of a successful landing a forlorn dream. Had we not had to go around, giving him an opportunity to see the gear, we probably would have crashed on landing.

I attempted to crank the wheel down manually. Sixty-six turns would do it, but it would not budge beyond fifty-six.

We tried sharp descents and sudden climbs to attempt to snap that pesky little wheel down, but it would not move.

Since a crash landing seemed an imminent possibility, we decided to return home for the event.

As we headed home, we began expelling fuel from the two auxiliary tanks to reduce the danger of fire as we crash-landed.

When we reached home, Jim talked to the Palm Beach Tower and Tilford's mechanic; then he called the manufacturer in Wichita, Kansas. All advice was gathered; then Jim faced all possibilities: a belly landing in the grass (our original decision); then ditching it in the ocean was considered; but finally we determined to attempt a two-wheel landing on the concrete runway, holding the nose off as long as possible, then taking the consequences of contact between aircraft and pavement.

By then we had just fifteen minutes of fuel left, so Jim brought the Cessna down for a practice run. There below us were the firetrucks, the ambulances, the sheriff's helicopter, and a back-up team. It was the most frightening encouragement I ever received!

Jim's voice interrupted my thoughts: "Jess, lead us in prayer."

I never prayed with such childlike simplicity before. "Lord, we men aboard this airplane belong to you. We have been on a mission for you. If you want to take us home to you, this life has been a great trip, and we've enjoyed every minute of it. If you spare us, we will know that you have something else for us to do. In either case we are yours. Now, Lord, I thank you for these four wonderful guys. They will always remain in my heart. Bless Jim as he does the best he can do to bring us down safely. We want you to know we love you with all our hearts. In Jesus' name. Amen."

All the fellows chimed in a quiet "Amen."

Then I did a silly thing. O. D. and I had worked together at First Baptist. I playfully blurted out "HALL!" and he came back with a flat and loud "What!" I turned and looked into his blessed face. Honestly, he looked like an angel (then—not now!).

And I quietly said, "Hall," and he softly answered, "What?"

I then shook Barry's hand, looked him in the eye and said, "I love you." He said, "I love you, too, Jess."

Then we were in the final approach. There below us coming up fast was the runway, the ambulances with the flashing lights, the firetrucks, the men in their fire-fighting suits, and the sheriff's hovering helicopter.

Each man buried his face in a pillow, bent over, and braced himself. The engines began sputtering. We were out of gas—and dropping fast!

Jim Baker cut all switches at about two hundred feet from impact, held the nose of the Cessna off the runway, and made contact at ninety miles an hour. The two wheels rolled down the runway, and we sat precariously balanced, waiting for the plane to nose down and possibly over.

Then the miracle of obesity happened.

For some almost unexplainable reason, the nose never went down; it went up, and the tail of the aircraft began dragging the ground!

"Praise God, we made it!" Barry shouted.

The most beautiful face in the world to me was Jim Baker's as great tears of gratitude and tension release ran down his cheeks. We were safe.

Forgive my laborious telling of this story. It may be of no interest to you whatsoever, but, believe me, it interests me greatly.

Are there any lessons to be drawn from this experience? For one thing, *we all face life's forced landings.* They come for everyone, and they will come for you.

This earth is a craft flying through space. It and all its inhabitants are determined to face a fateful moment when there is no evading, no postponing, no turning back.

For some of you, it comes *at the moment of death.* When that grim sarcasm comes to take you away, nothing you can do or say will change that moment when you must terminate your lease on life on earth.

A rich man once held onto me like a steel vise and screamed an almost mad cry, "I have plenty of money. You can have anything you ask—just make it possible for me to live here just one more year!"

The ultimate sacrilege would have been for me to promise him a minute. I am not Life's Pilot.

Another forced landing can occur before you die, and there are two versions of it: one for unbelievers and one for Christians. It is *the sin against the Holy Spirit.*

Yes, that old-fashioned doctrine preached a long time ago by old-fashioned preachers in old-fashioned days. I haven't read anything in the papers lately about the repeal of the consequences of the sin against the Holy Spirit.

You secular-minded people had better understand that the following words of Jesus are still in the Bible: "All manner of sin and blasphemy shall be forgiven men: but the blasphemy against the Holy Spirit shall not be forgiven men" (Matt. 12:31).

He also said: "He that shall blaspheme against the Holy Spirit hath never forgiveness, but is in danger of eternal damnation" (Mark 3:29).

Without going into infinite detail, what is involved in this awesome thought?

The Holy Spirit is the agent of conversion. He stirs the mind of man to think on his way, to consider being saved. The Holy Spirit reminds man of the guilt of sin and warns him that he should turn to God's forgiveness in Christ.

To ignore those subtle stirrings is to ensure your spiritual death. There is no way to escape if you ignore God's warning agent. So anything can be forgiven you if you will allow the Holy Spirit to introduce you to Jesus Christ, who has your personal salvation in his hands. If you will not allow that introduction to be made, you can never be forgiven, neither in this life nor in the life to come.

Do many people commit the sin against the Holy Spirit? I once said no, not many; but I am dreadfully afraid that the number committing this unforgivable sin is now in the many millions.

If you are living in an habitual state of *no* to Jesus Christ, you are committing the sin against the Holy Spirit.

A man can say no to God so long that it will become psychologically impossible to say yes to him. When it is no longer possible to say yes to Christ, there is no longer any reason for the Holy Spirit to continue to call.

> We used to sing an old song:
> There's a line that is drawn for rejecting our Lord
> When the call of the Spirit is lost,
> Have you counted, have you counted the cost.

Is it possible for a Christian to have the forced landing of the sin against the Holy Spirit, so that he loses his salvation? No. But there is another forced landing for the Christian who refuses to heed the Spirit's call to service. It is something to fear. Paul feared it.

If you as a Christian continue to refuse to obey God's clear commands to serve Him, *you can become a castaway.*

Look with serious eyes to 1 Corinthians 9:26. Here is Paul speaking of the race of life: "So fight I, not as one that beateth the air [a shadow boxer]. But I keep under my body and bring it unto subjection: lest that by any means . . . I myself should be a castaway."

A castaway. A has-been! A Christian once used greatly for the Lord now put on the shelf and left to collect dust as others less talented but more available are put in the forefront.

Look at the lost and found department of the Bible, Luke 15: *The lost son*—not available to fellowship with the Father.

The lost sheep—not available to provide wool to warm a cold world.

The lost coin—not available to be sent into circulation and spent for man's good.

The chief sin of the Christian is not some social or mildly moral matter. The chief sin is unavailability!

Be available, or be a castaway. Opt for availability.

We are like that coin—made to be sent into the world to circulate and be spent for the gospel's sake.

There is another forced landing this world yet faces: *the Second Coming of Jesus Christ.*

There is a rumor being circulated that Jess Moody doesn't believe in the Second Coming of Jesus. If anyone knows the source of that rumor, I want to meet those dear misinformed folks to tell them that I have believed and preached the Second Coming since the first sermon I preached, more than ten thousand sermons ago.

Their hang-up is the opposite of mine. I concentrate on *Who* is coming back, and they concentrate on *how* he is coming.

I wouldn't waste a minute debating the details of times and places. I am only interested in Jesus Christ, my wonderful Savior, coming back as the Lamb who became a Lion, the Servant who became a King, and One who died coming as the One with life in his hands!

You secular-minded people who make fun of all the little bumper stickers like "Guess Who's Coming Again?" or "In case of the Rapture, the driver will eject" make certain that you don't laugh yourself into hell.

Don't laugh at Christ's Second Coming lest you become one of the scoffers Peter talked about in 2 Peter 3:3–5, 7, 10, 17–18a.

There shall come in the last days scoffers . . . saying, Where is the promise of his coming? for . . . all things continue as they were from the beginning of creation. For this they willingly are ignorant of . . . But the heavens and the earth, which are now, by the same word are kept in store, reserved unto fire against the day of judgment and perdition of ungodly men. But the day of the Lord will come as a thief in the night; in which the heavens shall pass away with a great noise, and the elements shall melt with fervent heat, the earth also and the works that are in it shall be burned up . . . Ye therefore, beloved, seeing ye know these things . . . , beware lest ye also, being led away with the error of the wicked, fall from your stedfastness. But grow in grace, and in the knowledge of our Lord and Saviour Jesus Christ.

Yes, I believe he is coming again, and I believe we must be the kind of people who are ready for his coming.

We are not ready for his coming if we adopt the ascension robe mentality and spend all our time pouring over charts, maps, and newspapers, making a fetish of trying to pinpoint the exact time of his arrival.

A lot of people want to be at the airport when he arrives. I want to be far out in the midst of broken humanity. I want him to find me under the pile of shattered mankind, so identified with "the least of these" that it will be difficult to separate the point where their brokenness ends and my compassion begins.

Jesus told me where to be: reaching the lost sheep, giving a cup of cold water, going to the prison house, witnessing to an unsaved man, woman, or child.

If you want him to find you charting his course for him, reading maps, figuring who is the Antichrist, what 666 means, and tittling with tittles, and jotting jots, polishing the toes of Daniel, spinning the wheels of Ezekiel—you please help yourself. But I must warn you that when Jesus comes back, he will be greatly displeased with you for staying on the Mount of Transfiguration when there is a boy down in the valley who needs salvation, love, and healing.

What we are doing for Christ and his children is what he will ask about when he comes. "Inasmuch as you have done it [not] unto one of the least of these, my brothers, you have done it [not] unto me."

The forced landing of the Second Coming will catch more people by surprise than you can imagine.

How do you prepare for this forced landing life is bringing you?

1. *Consult your emergency manual.*

The minute Jim Baker realized we were in trouble, he reached into the glove compartment and pulled out a manual of emergency procedure. He and I, his nervous copilot, read as we have never read before the instructions in that manual.

You have an emergency manual called the Bible. You are facing a forced landing. Read it as though your life depends upon it, because it does.

2. *Get on the radio.*

Jim called everybody who had information that would help give as much advantage to us as possible.

Friend, if you are facing the forced landing of life, the radio is prayer. Call the Tower. Get all the help you can.

3. *Contact the Creator.*

We contacted the creator of the aircraft. Cessna, in Wichita, and talked to those who had made that nose wheel and asked what to do.

You can contact the Creator of your craft bound for a forced landing and talk to him. He will tell you what to do.

He will tell you to do what we knew we had to do. We knew we had to do two things!

4. *Trust the Pilot.*

We put all our trust, so far as the world is concerned, in Jim Baker, our pilot, and he brought that 320 Skyknight in for what old pilots at Tilford called the best landing in the history of Palm Beach International Airport.

Your pilot is Jesus Christ; you can trust Him.

"Trust the Lord Jesus Christ and you shall be saved."

5. *Commit your total future to the Lord.*

That's what we did that day. That's what you can do today. Will you do it?

FORTY-THREE

"I Saw Jesus, Sitting Right Here."

Cortland Myers, famous preacher and author, was traveling to a preaching opportunity.

Since it was the holiday season, the train was very crowded. There was hardly a seat available. Dr. Myers had been greatly overworked in his ministry, was bone-deep tired. He was looking forward to a quiet, gentle trip, with perhaps an hour or more of good, deep sleep.

He found a whole row of empty seats, breathed a prayer of gratitude, and stretched out to rest. He was nearly asleep when he felt a jarring kick in the small of his back. Looking around, he saw a bright-eyed child, her face filled with wonder, quite active and a little irritated. She seemed hyperactive, so she was kicking the seat in front of her, directly in the small of Dr. Myers's back.

It wasn't just one kick; it was six or eight of them.

Myers could see the whole trip as a series of kicks. As he

turned around, he wanted to shout, "Stop it! You're hurting my back!"

As he turned around, he noticed a tired, sad-eyed woman, doing her best to control not only the one little vitamin pill but two other hyperactives, three and four years of age.

He remembered how utterly weary his brood had made his wife when they were in that age range, so he whirled about, nose to eyes of the startled little girl. "Hey! How would you like to come up here and sit with me?"

Myers had bought a children's Wonder Book for his grand-children, so he thought that since he would get no sleep, he might as well check out the wonder power of the brightly col-ored children's book for its joy and amazement quotient.

"I have a great new book for boys and girls like you. Why don't all three of you come up here. I will read to you about some frogs, some dogs, some cats, and other glorious animals."

He had scored a hit.

They scrambled over and around the seat, and he found himself surrounded and bunched up against by three little eagers. They sat panting their child's breath in his face, their eyes dancing like the fabled sugarplum fairies.

He was much too tired to do the reading for very long, so he stretched out in the seat, and started reading very slowly and softly. This quietness only increased the sense of won-der, not to speak of the intensity of their interest, accompa-nied by growing volume of happiness and sheer, unalloyed child-joy.

He noticed the relief on the woman's face. It was but a moment until she was fast asleep.

Dr. Myers read of chocolate joys, lovely toys for girls and boys, filled with traveling joys. They rewarded him with laughter as he read of the cat chasing his own tail, not knowing it was his, so he bit it, sending cat screeches all over the place.

Myers found himself sounding much like Sir Anthony Hopkins, playing C. S. Lewis in *Shadowlands,* losing himself totally into the story. His voice would rise, when the story demanded it, and subside, like an ebb tide, when quietude was needed.

After he read for nearly an hour, the children had fallen asleep, dreaming of colored candies and ginger cookies shaped like the kittens in the story, as they leaped and bounded, playing with a ball of twine.

They dreamed of the gingerbread woman. *That's my mother, and the little children-cookies are Mary, Timmy, and I. We're about to go into the valley to play, running around Mother, holding her apron string, swinging on it until she falls, laughing and begging us to stop tickling her.*

They needed her, especially since their father had died in an automobile accident two years before.

She laughed so joyously in their dreams that the sound of her laughter awakened them. They had arrived at their destination. The conductor gathered them up, as the weary woman came out of her sleep with a start, picked up the bags, and herded them off the train.

They waved good-bye to Myers, calling him "The Reader Man."

Soon they were gone, and the train slowly pulled out of the station.

Myers sat in his now spacious area, ready for the rest but feeling good about having helped the sad-eyed woman to sleep a little, while he entertained the troops. A voice sounded in his ear. It had a thick Scottish accent, and it belonged to a handsome man, who had moved from his seat to talk with Myers.

He introduced himself and assured Myers that he would take but a moment.

"I've had a vision, I have!"

Myers, whose minister's collar gave him away, thought, *Oh, no, not one of those!* but hypocritically, he kept smiling and registered a look of interest in what the little Scot was saying.

"I saw the Lord Jesus, sitting right here beside you!"

Then, a wonder-look upon his face and trembling with emotion, he said, "The sad little woman was not their mother. She's the grandmother. The mother was lying in a coffin in the freight car up the train! Those children needed a Jesus right now, so the heavenly Father sent *you!*"

Myers said he walked up and down from one coach to another, looking to see if there might be other children who needed a "Reader Man."

FORTY-FOUR

Why I Am an Atheist About Religion

I must be an atheist about religion.

All religions are man-made, home brewed, tying human logic with a few altruistic truisms, then made pious.

It all starts when one person puts the religion down on paper, packs it with promises, espouses it, then sells it—and buyers are plentiful. A sucker for religion is born every ten seconds.

"Wait just a minute! Aren't you a preacher who has preached Christianity for more than fifty years?"

Yes, but I have come to the conclusion that one religion is as good, or bad, as the other. They are all man-made, codified, perfectly logical, offering nothing but false hope. I don't believe in religion. I hate it. It has killed and separated people into ridiculous little factions. There are perfectly religious people trying to make atom bombs and destroy the United States—and it is their religion that makes them do it.

I have a far better ethic than that. I believe that anyone who looks at religion with a hard investigative spirit will see the clay feet every time. Who needs it?

"Well, what do you believe?"

I believe that if I love my neighbor as myself, my neighbor will love me.

I believe that I should do good to anyone, especially those less fortunate, the down-and-outers, the least of society.

I believe that if I give a cup of cold water to a tired and thirsty person, I have done right.

I believe that I cannot be good enough, no matter how hard I try, to merit heaven. It is impossible for me to be that good. I have done too many bad, stupid things to be good enough, and there is no religion in the world that can solve that, so I say, "Let's quit wasting our time building false hopes on this religion stuff. If all I have to get my life squared away is to strain and struggle with all these religious rules, with the rope of regulations around my neck, then to heck with it."

As I said, I don't believe in religion. If religion is all I have, I must become an atheist.

Atheism is much more freed up than religion—and far more hopeful.

The only other hope that I see is Christianity.

"Whoa, whoa, whoa!" you say, "I thought you said that you didn't believe in any religion. Christianity is a religion. What sort of inconsistency is this?"

I believe I am still perfectly consistent in what I have said. I said I didn't have any religion, but I am a follower of Christ.

Christianity has never claimed that it was a religion. That is a name that secular people stuck onto Christianity. Religions are philosophies of life, rules to live by, codes to keep—all designed to tie us into a system.

There is no way to put Christ into that pluralistic alphabet soup of blending all religions into one.

This is all designed to make everybody happy, to feel good, to discharge religious duty, and not to offend anybody.

Let me make my point. There are only two choices in the world: atheism or following Jesus Christ.

Modern American, Hollywood-type pluralism is like John Nance Garner's definition of the vice presidency—"a bucket of warm spit."

I prefer a God who doesn't leave us all playing fifty questions, trying to define deity by some logical, philosophical guesswork, and the result always turns out to be that deity is what my psychological bent happens to be. If I am a left-brainer, I will manufacture a god who is a mass of algebraic equations, mixed with definitions more involved than a computer manual, not to be deviated from one jot.

If I am a right-brainer, my little mental manufactory will come out with a vague ethereal mist, to be defined by art, music, poetry, and literature. I can allude to my god, dance to his royal vagueness. Tell the world that I believe that with every drop of rain that falls a flower grows.

Down deep, we all know that this is divine drivel.

I can't waste my time doing obeisance to that great Wisp in the sky.

My whole life was changed when I walked out into a field just before sunrise and yelled, "I am an atheist if I have to sit around with other frustrates trying to figure out a jerk of a god who creates people, then refuses to define himself to them."

It is a mean god who won't clearly define himself. I don't like that kind of god, and I won't waste my time trying to figure him out.

What happens when a mass of people have it left to them to get a philosophy about God? They come out with a god like themselves. If they are contemplative, their god will come out like Buddha. If they are left-brained i-dotters and t-crossers, their god will come out like the rabid fundamentalists of all religions and raise the opposite of heaven with everyone who disagrees. They make great Muslims.

If their life is miserable, they will come up with a god with a juicy plan, with reincarnations and self-improvements like Hinduism.

Oh, there are infinite combinations that can leave you alone and let you figure it all out. Who knows, you might be able to end up like that great theologian Shirley MacLaine, on an umbilical cord from earth out among the planets!

Ultimately, you will be standing on a beach shouting, "I am god! I am god!" which is exactly where most religions end up.

You bet, I am an atheist about religion.

Make it clear: I am an atheist about religion.

I am a sold-out fan and follower of Jesus, who was a clear revelation of a kind God who chooses to define himself by becoming what we are so we could become like him.

He is the One who solves the three greatest problems of humankind.

And they are? Sin, sorrow, and death.

My atheism dies at the feet of the one God who loved us all enough to define himself instead of playing peekaboo with broken humanity.

FORTY-FIVE

The Shocking Story Behind Pearl Harbor

The Chapel by the Lake is a beauty spot among the lush greenery of the God-kissed garden called the Palm Beaches of south Florida. I designed it late one evening on the back of a paper napkin at a Howard Johnson restaurant.

The First Baptist Church of the Palm Beaches is a singularly beautiful location, directly on the water of the beautiful inter-coastal canal separating West Palm Beach from Palm Beach. Beside it a lovely bridge spans the intercoastal waters.

The church and Palm Beach Atlantic College are next to each other, and they face the Chapel by the Lake.

Directly across the intercoastal is a ship dock where the great yachts are moored. The rich and famous live aboard them. It was my joy to be the winter-pastor of many of them.

From our towers we rang the carillon bells, sounding some great hymn at dusk. It added a fragrance to the lovely floral nightfalls of that whole area. Hymns such as "How Great

Thou Art," "The Church's One Foundation," "Day Is Dying in the West," "Abide with Me," and many others bade the day farewell.

One morning I received a call from a gentleman named Eugene Wilson. He lived aboard a sumptious yacht at the Palm Beach Docks, directly across from our church and chapel.

"I want to thank you for the grand hymns that we hear each evening. It inspires us, and reminds us of our roots as Americans."

He invited me over to visit with him, which I gladly did. My old sailboat *Sailbad the Sinner* (Isn't that a great name for a poor preacher's seventy-year-old Herreschof?) registered a whimper in her rigging, a whisper of jealousy, as I left her to visit Eugene Wilson's grand vessel.

I was piped aboard by a handsome, elderly gentleman and his lovely wife, Ruth. I was greeted with such graciousness that they captured my heart immediately.

We sat at the stern of the lovely craft and the conversation quickly became a Babel of happy vocality, puntuated by laughter, happy stories, and coviviality. I learned so much that I shall forever treasure.

Eugene Wilson was a friend of two great flyers, Billy Mitchell and Charles Lindberg. In fact, he loaned me a personally autographed book, written by Lindberg, which I used as a basis for a sermon I preached at the Southern Baptist Pastor's Conference on "The Christian and War."

I learned that Eugene Wilson was one of America's first test pilots and tested the first radial engine for the navy. Those stories were charming, frightening, and consumingly interesting.

I was not quite prepared for the story he told me, perhaps the most interesting and insightful story I have ever heard.

Before I tell you his story, I must relate that Eugene Wilson was the top associate of James Forrestal, who was the head of aviation production in World War II. Wilson approached that war from a different perspective than any I had heard.

"War is a battle between the productive power of one nation against another. Wars are won in the assembly plants of the victor country."

Wilson went on to tell that in June of 1943, he brought a report to President Roosevelt that the United States would win the war in the spring of 1945 against Germany, and shortly after that a victory would be won over the Japanese.

This was the victory of America's productive power over the ability to produce products by the Axis powers. He was dead on.

But now, back to the most amazing story he told me as we sat at the bow of his yacht.

It was late November of 1931.

Wilson was serving under Admiral Adam "Bull" Reeves in Honolulu. Since he was so into aviation, Wilson was given a task that was looked upon by old navy as somewhat of a joke.

Commander Wilson was assigned the task of developing a strange naval concept called the "aircraft carrier," something called unthinkable, a pipe dream, and a waste of the navy's money, as the Old Guard said.

It was a clumsy-looking affair, with several long barges secured together to provide a runway.

Twenty-five biplanes, with bombs attached, were secured at one end of the runway, with some little hutlike cabins, which housed captain and crew.

It was a very un-navylike clumsy contraption.

Word came that Fleet A would leave Pearl Harbor on Wednesday in the last week of November, 1928. Fleet B would leave ten days later to seek to engage Fleet A in mock combat.

"Neither fleet wanted the albatross of the carrier around their necks, so they flipped a coin to see which poor sucker got the weird craft," Wilson chuckled.

Bull Reeves lost the toss, much to his dismay, so Fleet A pulled out, with that dead weight dragging along. About three days out, the captains of all the vessels met for dinner and a discussion about deployment against Fleet B, when they came out. Admiral Reeves was presiding at the discussion.

Commander Wilson requested the right to speak. "Gentlemen, I know you have been wondering what to do with our carrier. Some of the boys and I have come up with an idea."

All the others rolled their eyes, and they leaned back to hear the plan of Wilson and his merry men aboard the floating barges.

"Admiral, we were thinking that this Sunday morning, the men would be sleeping in after a night of carousing before Fleet B pulls out.

"We would like permission to bomb Fleet B in Pearl Harbor. Those flour bombs will register and mark our hits and our misses. We think we could stop them from even beginning their search-and-destroy mission."

The admiral smirked, "You men think those twenty-five kites could slip in there and catch them by surprise? That is such a dumb idea, it might work! We've got to find something for you airboys to do."

Permission was granted.

On the first Sunday in December of 1931, at 4:00 A.M. the engines leaped to life, and were warming up. One by one they wobbled down the unsure runway and lifted up into the night sky, journeying up into their formation.

At Pearl Harbor the crews of Fleet B were resting, sound asleep.

Suddenly alarms went off in every Fleet B vessel, men scurried around getting dressed to man their battle stations. It was too late.

The biplanes flew in low and dropped their dummy bombs on the decks of the great ships. Most of them were listed as having sank.

After the attack the biplanes landed at Hickam Field, which would have been rendered inoperable if the bombs had been real.

The pilots, at breakfast, were jubilant, hooting, howling, and punching one another.

One pilot spoke up. "Fellows, this is a great victory for aviation. We fooled them completely, No one saw us coming in! The only ones who saw us were those Japanese fishermen, going out on their morning run!"

FORTY-SIX

Douglas MacArthur's Greatest Story

We must get into the battlefield and off the bumper stickers! . . . or the world will think we are preaching "Ye Must Be Bored Again!"

When I preached the opening convocation at Annapolis, Chaplain O'Conner (the late Cardinal of New York) urged me to hear Douglas MacArthur as he spoke to the Quarterbacks Club. The General was a master verbal craftsman. He closed his magnificent address by telling the following beautiful, but gutsy, story.

The hordes of Chinese Communists swept across the hills of Korea in 1951. The secularists are swarming like killer bees at the turn of the millennium.

One of the greatest defensive ends in the history of the United States Military Academy was John Hall. In the Army-Navy game, the runners for the Navy tried flat-zone passes and wide sweeps. All to no avail.

John Hall seemed to be in on every play. So much so that they elected him honorary team captain.

Years later, when the Chinese troops were flooding over hill after hill in Korea, things got so bad that the Americans had to hold Hill 323—or a rout would occur. The battle raged for a day and a night. When gray dawn came, a reconnaissance crew was sent to investigate the results.

They were most interested in how the south end held, because it was the most strategic and most exposed. For thousands of yards there were dead Chinese and dead Americans.

They searched for the captain of that defensive position, Captain John Hill. They found him, mortally wounded, barely alive. He was lying face down in his own blood.

They turned him over.

His last words were: "What fools! To think that they could run around my end!"

Almighty God! They are swarming, and coming at us in droves. They shall not pass at this, our watch! Wake us, shake us, break us, and make us ready!

Almighty God . . . they shall not pass.

FORTY-SEVEN

The Inhabitant

I was driving down Matlock Avenue in Mansfield, Texas. Mansfield is the seventh fastest growing town in the state, with hundreds of houses, industrial buildings, schools, hospitals, and businesses rising up in what were farmlands a few years before.

I noted, only this morning, a giant crane, with its long arm reaching a hundred feet up the side of an edifice, rising skyward. I followed the long crane from its top, down to the motor which ran it. The churning engine seemed small compared to the long tentacle reaching up the building.

Even smaller than the engine was a tiny, by comparison, being, a human, sitting at the seat of control of the entire operation.

I thought, *How tiny is that person who, by a slight shift of a gear, can move hundreds of tons of steel to do his bidding.*

Then I thought, *There is an even more tiny organ, commanding the human body to do its bidding.*

That tiny organ is the brain of the whole operation. The brain instructs the hand to move to the gear, then to the throttle, and the massive engine roars its power relay system to the far extremity of the crane—and it responds with almost instant obedience.

That giant concept crowded my brain, and I thought, *The brain controls almost everything in this world.*

All advertising, teaching, preaching, and every conceivable communication technique is designed to cause the brain to cause the body to cause whatever instrument of communication to act according to the will of a small organ, not larger than two clinched fists—the little human brain!

Then, my mind began to respond to the idea that there is a God force and a counter-God force competing for the attention of that tiny organ.

The brain of a bombardier aboard the *Enola Gay* released the bomb that blew away Hiroshima. Just think—an instrument no larger than a grapefruit designed, built the aircraft and the bomb, and released it to eliminate a city!

Whatever intelligent forces there are in this universe must be striving by all means to control that small organ. Evil does not desire to control the world; it merely wishes to control the small brain, and the world is in its control.

Listening late at night to early A.M. radio, I heard a story that sent chills throughout my body. Carl Zimmer, author of a chilling book, *Parasite Rex,* told the story of a rapidly growing parasite inside a crab's body, feeding off the muscles of the crab, eating everything but the brain. The parasite then controls the brain, causing the crab to continue to live . . . *with a life other than its own, causing the crab to do its bidding. An alien at its command post!*

The implications of the story chilled my very being. Is there a Parasite Rex, plotting, planning a devious entrance into the control chamber of my central self?

Is there a mind, other than the mind of God or man, that debates, fights, cons, chills, emotes, and attempts gently to steal away the wheel of the will of a human being's control center?

Could that be the reason Paul said, "We wrestle not against flesh and blood, but against powers" (Eph. 6:12)?

Could that be the reason he insisted, "Let this mind be in you, which was also in Christ Jesus" (Phil. 2:5)?

Could that be the reason he said, "Be sober, be vigilant, because your adversary the devil, . . . walketh about . . . *seeking whom he may devour*" (1 Pet. 5:8, italics added)?

Could there be a universal *Parasite Rex?*

FORTY-EIGHT

God's Sense of Humor

One day a group of scientists got together and decided that man had come a long way and no longer needed God. So they picked one scientist to go tell him they were finished with him.

The scientist walked up to God and said, "God, we've decided that we no longer need you. We're to the point that we can clone people and do many miraculous things, so why don't you just go on and get lost."

God listened patiently and kindly After the scientist finished talking, God said, "Very well, how about this? Let's have a man-making contest." To which the scientist replied, "OK, great!"

But God added, "Now, we're going to do this just like I did back in the old days with Adam."

The scientist said, "Sure, no problem," and bent down and grabbed himself a handful of dirt.

God looked at him and said, "No, no, no. You go make your own dirt!"

FORTY-NINE

Chariots of Fire II

I was asked to be one of the research writers for the movie "Chariots of Fire II." The film never came about, for reasons best not discussed here.

During my research I discovered an experience, added a small dose of imagination, and the following story flowed through my fingers onto the keyboard.

Eric Littel was a Christian, the son of a Scottish missionary family, and won the gold medal for the two-hundred-meter run in the 1924 Olympics.

Harold Abrahams was Jewish. He won the gold medal for the one-hundred-meter run.

All England was most proud of both of them.

One day Harold Abrahams and Eric Littel were training younger Olympic aspirants in the art of relay running, and especially concentrating on passing the baton.

Littel came privately to Abrahams and spoke in his gentle

manner: "Mr. Abrahams, I have wonderful news. I have been accepted to go back to China as a missionary."

Littel spent his childhood in China and was eager to return.

"But, you are needed *here!*" Abrahams didn't show the least bit of understanding. It was the wasting of a life, as he saw it.

Littel dropped all formalities, so typical of Oxford and Cambridge men. "Harold, before I go, I want to offer you the baton of faith in Jesus Christ." He held up the baton.

Abrahams refused to take it that day. Many years later Abrahams was a successful business executive and was an outstanding leader and supporter of track and field. One day he was in his study in his palatial home. His actress wife came into the room.

"Harold, I just received the news that Mr. Littel died in a concentration camp in China. It was a brain tumor. I should think you would want to be alone for awhile."

Abrahams sat for a long period looking into the fire. Suddenly the very flesh on the back of his neck began to tighten. A memory was directly behind him. He looked over his shoulder. His imagination beheld the sight of that unorthodox young Scot running full tilt, stretching and straining—and in his hand was *the baton!* Abrahams's hand slowly fell to his side, as he reached back to take the baton of faith.

A young British man in our church in California, Robert Abrahams, was Harold's nephew. He reported that, indeed, Abrahams became a believer. He was given a Christian burial, as seen in the film *Chariots of Fire*.

If that is so, he took the baton! You are the long line of baton passers who have relayed from family to family the

Christian message, and that has made the message move from nation to nation and from heart to heart. From father to son, from mother to daughter, from family to family . . . the beat goes on!

FIFTY

For All of Us in a Hurry

Jack took a long look at his speedometer before slowing down: seventy-three in a fifty-five zone. Fourth time in as many months. How could a guy get caught so often?

When his car had slowed to ten miles an hour, Jack pulled over, but only partially. Let the cop worry about the potential traffic hazard. Maybe some other car will tweak his backside with a mirror. The cop was stepping out of his car, the big pad in hand.

Bob? Bob from church? Jack sank farther into his trench coat. This was worse than the coming ticket. A Christian cop catching a guy from his own church. A guy who happened to be a little anxious to get home after a long day at the office. A guy he was about to play golf with tomorrow!

Jumping out of the car, he approached a man he saw every Sunday, a man he'd never seen in uniform.

"Hi, Bob. Fancy meeting you like this."

"Hello, Jack." No smile.

"Guess you caught me red-handed in a rush to see my wife and kids."

"Yeah, I guess." Bob seemed uncertain. Good.

"I've seen some long days at the office lately. I'm afraid I bent the rules a bit—just this once." Jack toed at a pebble on the pavement. "Diane said something about roast beef and potatoes tonight. Know what I mean?"

"I know what you mean. I also know that you have a reputation in our precinct."

Ouch! This was not going in the right direction. Time to change tactics.

"What'd you clock me at?"

"Seventy-one. Would you sit back in your car, please?"

"Now wait a minute here, Bob. I checked as soon as I saw you. I was barely nudging sixty-five." The lie seemed to come easier with every ticket.

"Please, Jack, in the car."

Flustered, Jack hunched himself through the still-open door. Slamming it shut, he stared at the dashboard. He was in no rush to open the window. The minutes ticked by. Bob scribbled away on the pad. Why hadn't he asked for a driver's license?

Whatever the reason, it would be a month of Sundays before Jack ever sat in church near this cop again.

A tap on the door jerked his head to the left. There was Bob, a folded paper in hand. Jack rolled down the window a mere two inches, just enough room for Bob to pass him the slip.

"Thanks." Jack could not quite keep the sneer out of his voice. Bob returned to his car without a word. Jack watched his retreat in the mirror. Jack unfolded the sheet of paper. How much was this one going to cost?

Wait a minute. What was this? Some kind of joke? Certainly not a ticket. Jack began to read:

Dear Jack,

Once upon a time I had a daughter. She was six when killed by a car. You guessed it—a speeding driver. A fine and three months in jail, and the man was free. Free to hug his daughters. All three of them. I only had one, and I'm going to have to wait until heaven before I can ever hug her again. A thousand times I've tried to forgive that man. A thousand times I thought I had. Maybe I did, but I need to do it again. Even now . . . Pray for me. And be careful. My son is all I have left. Bob

Jack twisted around in time to see Bob's car pull away and head down the road. Jack watched until it disappeared. A full fifteen minutes later, he too, pulled away and drove slowly home, praying for forgiveness and hugging a surprised wife and kids when he arrived.

Life is precious. Handle with care.

FIFTY-ONE

The Carameling of the Church

Now that I am leaning slightly toward Beulah Land, and the years have stealthily crept up on me and suddenly attacked me on the blind side, I have begun to research what aging really is and how to slow it down.

I know that I will be ready and eager to meet my escort angel, whom I call "Goodwood" in some of my other and more fanciful writings.

The process of how God will usher me into the heavenly realms doesn't cause a second's pause; but the prospect is beaming bright, and the joy of the arrival where there is no night causes a kind of "Glory Anticipation" to flood my being.

For this reason, I have become intrigued with how science approaches old age, or senescence, they call it. But the secular interpretation of aging does swamp my mind at times; and I do want to live here at least another fifty years or more, mainly because of McPatland's claim that all knowledge is now doubling every ten years and will progress until it doubles every ninety days. I, quite simply, want to see what will transpire in the next six decades; ergo, I seek to know about the prospect of earth days, yet to be.

One earth day drops off the calendar every twenty-four hours. Science has been searching for the power to extend life; and in doing so, they have stumbled upon some amazing facts about senescence, aging.

There are many titles for aging, and a massive scientific onslaught has stormed the nooks and crannies of the intellectual world to seek the fountain of youth.

THE PONCE PRINCIPLE

I call it *The Ponce Principle*. Ponce de Leon sought the fountain of youth.

It is a fact of science that cells will duplicate just so many times. Some scientists say that usually a cell will duplicate perhaps eighty to one hundred times, then suddenly, it stops. It just quits. Death is the refusal of cells to change any more.

CARAMELING

As it draws nearer the quitting time, there seems to be a gooing up of the cells. Thus, they have become sticky, emitting a substance that makes them cluster. This is called "carameling."

Like caramel candy, the gooing up of the stickiness, everything slows down: response, speed, thinking, dexterity, and reproducing. One knows death is coming when the gooing-up becomes apparent. This is called senescence, the adverse changes that occur during the aging of any organism.

The most important indicator that death is coming is the increasing refusal of cells to change. It means death is much nearer, speeding toward the goo.

Exercise breaks up the gooing somewhat and gives a better quality of life—but not necessarily much longer life.

Church Carameling

Apply all this to a church.

Each organization is a cell in a church. The signs that a church is entering into senescence are the slowing of the reproduction of the cells, the clustering and gooing up of the cells. These cells are highly resistant to change.

"I'm a choir member (a cell), and I don't like these changes that are taking place (reproduction resistance). This new music isn't dignified and stately (goo), and I want this minister of music (stimulant to cell reproduction) out of here!"

Out with the minister of music; in with the goo!

"I am a member of the deacons (a cell); and they are attempting to set up a rotating board (cell reproduction); and I want those people stopped (reproduction slowdown). We can stop it if all of us deacons will stick together. We have a nice, good sweet fellowship in our board; and it doesn't need to be changed (carameling)!"

Run such a test on every committee, board, class, seminar, Bible teaching unit, music group, elders, deacons, stewards, finance. I know of no church anywhere in the world that is gooed and growing at the same time.

It is just a matter of time. Look at Christianity in England.

It was thriving at a furious pace 150 years ago. Look at Spurgeon's Metropolitan Church in London in the 1870s. The cells were hot, the growth was not only a result of Spurgeon's dynamic preaching; but the deacons, the outreach to young men and women, the classes—all were also dynamically alive and vibrant. Reproduction was everywhere.

Seventy years later I was asked by Graham Scroggie, the pastor, to preach there. Perhaps there were two hundred people present. They had a lockstep, veddy British, most rutualistic (that is from the Greek word *rut*) service. Graham Scroggie was a better Bible interpreter than Spurgeon ever dreamed of being.

But the usual crowd, moved by habituality (Did I just coin a new word?!), labored through the service.

After the mosaic, prosaic worship hour, Dr. Scroggie and I went out to dinner.

We were having a most alert, alive, and joyous discussion, sharing wondrous stories about the ministry. In the midst of the most delightful discussion, Scroggie suddenly grew quiet, almost pensive, almost sorrowful. Thoughtlessly, I had just recounted a preaching experience at the First Baptist Church of Dallas, Texas, with the great Dr. W. A. Criswell. I had mentioned their glorious music, the throngs packing the pews with alert, happy people. Looking back, it was quite thoughtless of me to do it, in the light of the experience of preaching to two hundred souls in the Metropolitan Chapel.

Scroggie became soft of speech. "Jess, did you notice the portly old gentleman, standing back in the shadows?"

"No, Dr. Scroggie, I don't seem to recall seeing such a person."

"If you had noticed him, you would have seen something unusual. He attends every service, always stands back in the shadows, and always weeps during the service."

My curiosity was peaked. "Who is he?" I asked.

"It was the ghost of Charles Haddon Spurgeon! He wept at what had happened to his church."

Spurgeon was weeping at what the carameling goo can do!

When the Holy Spirit came down at Pentecost, everybody became ungooed—except the gooed-up-by-tradition Pharisees.

Where the Holy Spirit reigns, there is a rapid speedup of cell reproduction.

The only intolerance one will find at that church is an angry, almost forceful, resistance toward those who try to slow up change! They literally throw out the goo-impeders.

Dr. Cho's church in Korea is made up of a complete unfettering of cell reproduction; and that church now has nearly eight hundred thousand members!

To build a church that is topless(!), with reference to growth, there must be an absolute commitment to cell reproduction. Ungooed! Decaramelized! Revival!

FIFTY-TWO

The Widow

To Doris:

The trail is longer behind me.
The steps are fewer ahead.
What steps I take in days to come
Must be grand in Christ's stead.

Age often sends countercurrents
To hate, hurts, anger, and fear.
The learning curve brings deterrents
Memories beautiful, ling'ring, dear.

I light a candle, shimmering yellow,
Reflecting the faded picture
Of him when he was my "fellow,"
His personality just my mixture.

His Bible with scribblings like a child,
Written in wavering old man's scrawl
About the gentle Jesus, meek and mild,
Who loved us and died for one and all.

And then I find his markings, let's see:
Jesus said, "I'm leaving now; I'll come for you."
John fourteen, verses one through three,
Jesus came for him, and made him new!

And when that happens, my heart will beat,
And my tired weak'ning eyes shall see
The one in the candlelit picture.
Bright, alive, happy—and with me!

FIFTY-THREE

Butch O'Hare

World War II produced many heroes. One such man was Butch O'Hare. He was a fighter pilot assigned to an aircraft carrier in the South Pacific. One day his entire squadron was sent on a mission. After he was airborne, he looked at his fuel gauge and realized that someone had forgotten to top off his fuel tank. He would not have enough fuel to complete his mission and get back to his ship. His flight leader told him to return to the carrier. Reluctantly he dropped out of formation and headed back to the fleet.

As he was returning to the mother ship, he saw something that turned his blood cold. A squadron of Japanese Zeroes was speeding its way toward the American fleet. The American fighters were gone on a sortie, and the fleet was all but defenseless. He couldn't reach his squadron and bring them back in time to save the fleet. Nor could he warn the fleet of the approaching danger. There was only one thing to do. He must somehow divert them from the fleet.

Laying aside all thoughts of personal safety, he dove into the formation of Japanese planes. Wing-mounted 50 calibers blazed as he charged in, attacking one surprised enemy plane and then another. Butch wove in and out of the now broken formation and fired at as many planes as possible until finally all his ammunition was spent. Undaunted, he continued the assault. He dove at the Zeroes, trying at least to clip off a wing or tail in hopes of damaging as many enemy planes as possible and rendering them unfit to fly. He was desperate to do anything he could to keep them from reaching the American ships. Finally, the exasperated Japanese squadron took off in another direction.

Deeply relieved, Butch O'Hare and his tattered fighter limped back to the carrier. Upon arrival he reported in and related the event surrounding his return. The film from the camera mounted on his plane told the tale. It showed the extent of Butch's daring attempt to protect his fleet. He was recognized as a hero and given one of the nation's highest military honors.

Today, O'Hare Airport in Chicago is named in tribute to the courage of this great man.

****

Some years earlier there was a man in Chicago called Easy Eddie. At that time Al Capone virtually owned the city. Capone wasn't famous for anything heroic. His exploits were anything but praiseworthy. He was, however, notorious for enmeshing the city of Chicago in everything from bootlegged booze and prostitution to murder.

Easy Eddie was Capone's lawyer and for a good reason. He was very good! In fact, his skill at legal maneuvering kept Big Al out of jail for a long time. To show his appreciation, Capone paid him very well. Not only was the money big, but Eddie also got special dividends. For instance, he and his family occupied a fenced-in mansion with live-in help and all of the conveniences of the day. The estate was so large that it filled an entire Chicago city block. Yes, Eddie lived the high life of the Chicago mob and gave little consideration to the atrocities that went on around him.

Eddie did have one soft spot, however. He had a son that he loved dearly. Eddie saw to it that his young son had the best of everything—clothes, cars, and a good education. Nothing was withheld. Price was no object.

And, despite his involvement with organized crime, Eddie even tried to teach his son right from wrong. Yes, Eddie tried to teach his son to rise above his own sordid life. He wanted him to be a better man than he was.

Yet, with all his wealth and influence, there were two things that Eddie couldn't give his son. Two things that Eddie sacrificed to the Capone mob that he could not pass on to his beloved son, a good name and a good example.

One day Easy Eddie reached a difficult decision. Offering his son a good name was far more important than all the riches he could lavish on him. He had to rectify all the wrong that he had done. He would go to the authorities and tell the truth about "Scar-face" Al Capone. He would try to clean up his tarnished name and offer his son some semblance of integrity. To do this he would have to testify against the mob, and he knew that the cost would be great. But more than anything, he wanted to be an example to his son. He wanted to do his best to make restoration and hopefully have a good name to leave his son.

So he testified.

Within the year Easy Eddie's life ended in a blaze of gunfire on a lonely Chicago street. He had given his son the greatest gift he had to offer at the greatest price he would ever pay.

So what do these two stories have to do with one another?

Butch O'Hare was Easy Eddie's son.

Readers love *Club Sandwich*

by Jess Moody

"'The Day I Slept with the Pope,' 'Rose Kennedy's Manger Heart,' 'My Mother's Last Date with Burt Reynolds,' and 'The Day Lenin and I Handed Out Tracts' had me laughing, crying, and moved to God."

—Brent Smith, Youngstown, OH

"We bought seven copies for friends." —

Kimberling City, MO

"Roger Cunningham *bought fifty copies* to give to friends, family, and employees for Christmas. Etta Mae Moseley bought fifteen copies."

—Don Harp, FL

"This book nearly destroyed my family. We were fighting over it!"

—Brent Smith, Youngstown, OH

"We offered it in our church and it sold out in ten minutes."
—Dan Griffin, Christ Fellowship Baptist Church,
Arlington, TX

"I started reading it as soon as I received it, and I read the whole thing without sitting down!"

—Ken Sharp

"Jess Moody, always the master of the spoken word, here illustrates his mastery of the English language in his writings also . . . humorous, always evoking a smile or a laugh that cannot be contained."

—S. L. Harris, TX

"I am a fan of Jess Moody, and this is must reading!"
—Randy Quaid, CA

"Fun to read."

—Gail Thompkins, AR

"Downright funny and inspirational, too."
—Gloria Roach, Dallas, TX

"With the tragedy and cruelty that we hear so much in the media, this collection is a refreshing look at the world."
—Jeanne Short, Springdale, AR

"I was on every page, then I found a whole chapter about me!"
—Don Phillips, casting director, Hollywood, CA